Treasures in Truth

Quotes to Nourish Your Soul

JOHN MICHAEL MOONEY

INNERVISIONS
PUBLICATIONS

Coloma, California

Published by Innervisions Publications
P. O. Box 213, Coloma, CA 95613

Editors: Gina Giacomini, Ellen Kleiner
Book cover design: Janice St. Marie
Dove artwork © Kevin Carden, Dreamstime.com

First Edition

While every effort has been made to ensure the reliability of the information presented in this publication, the author does not guarantee the accuracy of the data contained herein and accepts no payment for listing; inclusion of any organization, agency, institution, publication or individual does not imply endorsement of the editors or publisher.

Publisher's Cataloging-in-Publication Data
Mooney, John Michael.
Treasures in truth : quotes to nourish your soul / John Michael Mooney.
Ist edition. | Coloma, CA : Innervisions, 2017.
LCCN 2016954361 | ISBN 978-0-9669427-3-6 (hardcover)
LCSH: Quotations, English. | Inspiration--Quotations, maxims, etc. | Motivation
(Psychology)--Quotations, maxims, etc. | Self-actualization (Psychology) | BISAC: REFERENCE /
Quotations. | BODY, MIND & SPIRIT / Inspiration & Personal Growth.
LCC PN6081 .M519 2017 (print)

1 3 5 7 9 10 8 6 4 2

I dedicate this book to my late friend and high school coach, Lou Ruiz—a man of great wisdom who left his imprint of kindness upon my life.

ACKNOWLEDGMENTS

With special thanks to:

My mother-in-law, Rhea Landes, the kindest
person I know

My beautiful wife, Ellen; my children, Matt,
Brent and Victoria and my grandson, Matthew
Abraham who give me unbelievable happiness

Cherilyn Bolton, for her friendship, help and
support over the last thirty-four years

Randy Ricklieb and Jerry Walls, who are closer
to me than any brothers

Gina Giacomini, my book consultant and friend

CONTENTS

PREFACE

About thirty years ago I started reading the Book of Proverbs daily. Over time, I came across quotes from other wisdom traditions that spoke to my soul. To ensure I would remember these writings, I wrote them in between the proverbs in my Bible, revisiting them faithfully. Soon the Book of Proverbs was completely filled so I began writing them between the Book of Psalms verses. Eventually it dawned on me that if anything happened to my Bible, this entire collection of wisdom would be lost forever—a realization that prompted me to create *Treasures in Truth*. In reflection, I realized my spirit was the driving force behind this anthology of quotations.

The following is a tour guide to this book which reflects its origin. Each section, focusing on a theme of its own, opens with a psalm, followed by quotes that offer the reader a richer, deeper meaning on the topic—at times even challenging the meanings of the different sayings.

The range of authors, past and present, shows how universal truths transcend time, space and cultures.

Use this book in any way you wish. Choose a theme each day that is relevant to you or, alternatively, follow the sequence presented in the book. Whatever approach you decide upon, I encourage you to read a theme a day for one month and discover how their wisdom nourishes and brings peace to your soul. May *Treasures in Truth* help you greet every challenge in life as a blessing in disguise.

The following abbreviations identify the Bible sources in this book:

American Standard Version: ASV
English Standard Version: ESV
Good News Translation: GNT
Holman Christian Standard Bible: HCSB
King James Bible: KJB
New American Standard Bible: NASB
New International Version: NIV
New Living Translation: NLT

ABUNDANCE

*But the meek shall inherit the land and delight
themselves in abundant peace.*
—Psalm 37:11 ESV

*An abundant life is one in which I am free to do
what I want, when I want, with no restrictions,
deadlines or schedules.*
—Wayne W. Dyer

*Abundance is about being rich with or without
money.*
—Suze Orman

*It is not how much we have, but how much we
enjoy, that makes happiness.*
—Charles H. Spurgeon

Giving is the secret of abundance.
—Swami Sivananda

Gratitude is the open door to abundance.
—Yogi Bhajan

*When you are grateful, fear disappears and abun-
dance appears.*
—Tony Robbins

You pray in your distress and in your need; would that you might also pray in the fullness of your joy and in your days of abundance.
—Kahlil Gibran

Riches are not from an abundance of worldly goods, but from a contented mind.
—Muhammad

Not what we have but what we enjoy, constitutes abundance.
—Epicurus

Accumulation of wealth for the sake of wealth alone is self-defeating.
—Jon Huntsman

The test of our progress is not whether we add more to the abundance of those who have much, it is whether we provide enough to those who have little.
—Franklin D. Roosevelt

To live a pure unselfish life, one must count nothing as one's own in the midst of abundance.
—Buddha

Abundance is a process of letting go; that which is empty can receive.
—Bryant H. McGill

Thank God my parents had an abundance of patience.
—Lexa Doig

ACTION

They, too, observed the Lord's power in action,
His impressive works on the deepest seas.
                                            —Psalm 107:24 NLT

Do not wait to strike till the iron is hot; but make it hot by striking.
                                            —William B. Yeats

The ancestor of every action is a thought.
                                            —Ralph Waldo Emerson

Ideas without action are worthless.
                                            —Helen Keller

Fear has a hard time coexisting with action.
                                            —Steve Chandler

You can't move people to action unless you move them with emotion; the heart comes before the head.
                                            —John C. Maxwell

Never confuse movement with action.
                                            —Ernest Hemmingway

Action is the foundational key to all success.
                                            —Pablo Picasso

Vision without action is a daydream. Action without vision is a nightmare.
> —Japanese Proverb

In order to carry a positive action we must develop here a positive vision.
> —Dalai Lama

Vision without action is merely a dream. Action without vision just passes the time. Vision with action can change the world.
> —Joel A. Barker

Repetition is the mother of learning, the father of action, which makes it the architect of accomplishment.
> —Zig Ziglar

If there is something wrong, then those who have the ability to take action have the responsibility to take action.
> —Thomas Jefferson

In any moment of decision, the best thing you can do is the right thing, the next best thing is the wrong thing, and the worst thing you can do is nothing.
> —Theodore Roosevelt

Words may show a man's wit, but actions his meaning.
> —Benjamin Franklin

Thoughts lead to feelings. Feelings lead to actions. Actions lead to results.
—T. Harv Eker

Think like a man of action, act like a man of thought.
—Henry Bergson

Follow effective action with quiet reflection. From the quiet reflection will come even more effective action.
—Peter Drucker

We receive enlightenment only in proportion as we give ourselves more and more completely to God by humble submission and love. We do not first see, then act; we act and then see.
—Thomas Merton

Religion has two types, the do and the done.
—John M. Mooney

The fruit of love is service which is compassion in action. Religion has nothing to do with compassion. It is our love for God created for the sole purpose to love and to be loved.
—Mother Teresa

Getting old is not about age, it's about a lack of movement. And the ultimate lack of movement is death.
—Tony Robbins

BELIEF

I believe that I shall look upon the Lord's goodness while I am here in the land of the living.
—Psalm 27:13 ESV

All the great ages have been ages of belief.
—Ralph Waldo Emerson

God is always previous.
—Baron Friedrich
von Hügel

Many Christians today want religious experience without religious belief.
—John M. Mooney

God wounds us through the law in order to heal us through the gospel.
—Karl L. Barth

At the root of the Christian life lies in the belief of the invisible. The object of the Christian's faith is unseen reality.
—A. W. Tozer

Nothing Jesus ever said was initiated by common sense, but rather by 'revelation sense.'
—Celta Kirkland

Believe. Have faith. Trust God.
                    —Anonymous

The four most dangerous words regarding the church are: if we can just.
                    —Jonathan Fisk

If you believe what you like in the gospels and reject what you don't like, it is not the gospel you believe in, but yourself.
                    —St. Augustine

When we believe and act upon some sin in our life, we begin to experience the miracle when the desire for that habit is taken away and the power of sin is broken.
                    —C. S. Lewis

The church that doesn't want to grow is saying to the world, 'Go to hell.'
                    —Rick Warren

Ask a person to say, 'Jesus Christ is my Lord and Savior.' The unsaved cannot say this.
                    —John M. Mooney

You become what the most important person in your life thinks you are (wife, father, boss, etc).
                    —Philip Yancey

Whether you think you can, or think you can't, you're right.
                    —Henry Ford

Believe you can and you're halfway there.
—Theodore Roosevelt

A wise man proportions his belief to the evidence.
—David Hume

One person with a belief is equal to ninety-nine who only have interests.
—John Stuart Mill

The will to do springs from the knowledge that we can do.
—James Allen

If they don't stand for nothing, they will fall for anything.
—Gordon A. Eadie

A thing is not necessarily true because a man dies for it.
—Oscar Wilde

I had therefore to remove knowledge, in order to make room for belief.
—Immanuel Kant

Reality is that which, when you stop believing in it, doesn't go away.
—Philip K. Dick

Believe that life is worth living and your belief will help create the fact.
—William James

BLESSING

Taste and see that the Lord is good; blessed is the one who takes refuge in Him.
                              —Psalm 34:8 NIV

I feel I'm very blessed. But with great blessings come great responsibility.
                              —Kanye West

Every burden is a blessing.
                              —Walt Kelly

Sanctification means nothing less than the holiness of Jesus becoming mine and being exhibited in my life.
                              —Oswald Chambers

Our supreme model for unity is the Trinity.
                              —Rick Warren

How can God bless you if you don't love and bless your wife?
                              —John M. Mooney

The unthankful heart discovers no mercies; but the thankful heart...so it will find, in every hour, some heavenly blessings.
                              —Henry Ward Beecher

Man's chief end is to glorify God and to enjoy Him forever.

—Westminster Shorter Catechism

The laws of God are really his gifts to us.
—John M. Mooney

I think in every lesson there's a blessing, and there's so many blessings from all the lessons I've had to go through in life.
—Alonzo Mourning Jr.

Those blessings are sweetest that are won by prayer and worn with thanks.
—Thomas Goodwin

When we lose one blessing, another is often most unexpectedly given in its place.
—C. S. Lewis

An early morning walk is a blessing for the whole day.

—Henry David Thoreau

Reflect upon your present blessings—of which every man has many—not on your past misfortunes, of which all men have some.
—Charles Dickens

A blessing is a circle of light drawn around a person to protect, heal and strengthen.
—John O'Donohue

CHANGE

Therefore we will not fear, though the earth do change, and though the mountains be shaken into the heart of seas.
—Psalm 46:2 ASV

Be the change you wish to see in the world.
—Mahatma Gandhi

Sometimes in the winds of change, we find our true direction.
—Unknown

You cannot change your destination overnight, but you can change your direction.
—Jim Rohn

All change is not growth, as all movement is not forward.
—Ellen Glasgow

If you want to change your life, begin by changing your words.
—Robert Kiyosaki

Change your thoughts and you change your world.
—Norman Vincent Peale

Caesar sought to change man by changing institutions. Jesus Christ sought to change institutions by changing men.
                                   —Will Durant

As long as you're moving, it will take God less energy to change your direction.
                                   —Henry Cloud

History proves one thing: every empire comes to an end.
                                   —Steven A. Campos

When dictatorship is a fact, revolution becomes a right.
                                   —Victor Hugo

Change is the law of life. And those who look only to the past or present are certain to miss the future.
                                   —John F. Kennedy

Virtually everything we do is to change the way we feel.
                                   —Tony Robbins

Everyone thinks about changing the world, but no one thinks of changing himself.
                                   —Leo Tolstoy

Yesterday I was clever, so I wanted to change the world. Today I am wise, so I am changing myself.
                                   —Rumi

When we are no longer able to change a situation—we are challenged to change ourselves.
　　　　　—Viktor E. Frankl

Progress is impossible without change, and those who cannot change their minds cannot change anything.
　　　　　—George Bernard Shaw

The only way to make sense out of change is to plunge into it, move with it, and join the dance.
　　　　　—Alan Watts

Growth means change and change involves risk, stepping from the known to the unknown.
　　　　　—George Shinn

We cannot become what we need to be by remaining what we are.
　　　　　—Max De Pree

If you don't like something, change it. If you can't change it, change your attitude.
　　　　　—Maya Angelou

Never believe that a few caring people can't change the world. For, indeed, that's all who ever have.
　　　　　—Margaret Mead

All is connected...no one thing can change by itself.
　　　　　—Paul Hawken

CHARACTER

He revealed His character to Moses, and His deeds to the people of Israel.

—Psalm 103: 7 NLT

Try not to be a man of success, but rather try to be a man of value.

—Albert Einstein

God is much more concerned about your character than your career, because you will take your character into eternity, but not your career.

—Rick Warren

A man's character is his guardian divinity.

—Heraclitus

It is not what we do that determines who we are; it is who we are that determines what we do.

—Neil T. Anderson

I am no bird; and no net ensnares me: I am a free human being with an independent will.

—Charlotte Brontë

A man wrapped up in himself makes a very small bundle.

—Benjamin Franklin

Sports do not build character. They reveal it.
—Heywood Hale Brown

What happens to you speaks of your circumstances, what happens in you speaks of your character. And what happens through you speaks of your charisma.

—John C. Maxwell

Leadership is a matter of having people look at you and gain confidence, seeing how you react. If you are in control, they are in control.
—Tom Landry

Leaders are like eagles...they don't flock, you'll find them one at a time.

—Knute Rockne

The world has always been betrayed by decent men with bad ideals.

—Sidney J. Harris

The godlessness round about us, that which others do and say is never the worst thing. The worst dwells within ourselves.

—Bo Giertz

Remember what lust is—'I must have it now.'
—Oswald Chambers

Money cannot buy peace of mind. It cannot heal ruptured relationships or build meaning into a life that has none.

—Richard M. Devos

A great man shows his greatness by the way he treats little men.
—Thomas Carlyle

Reputation is made in a moment; character is built in a lifetime.
—William Hersey Davis

Ability can take you to the top, but it takes character to keep you there.
—John Wooden

Remember that your character is the sum total of your habits.
—Rick Warren

Tell me what you eat and I will tell you what you are.
—Brillat Savarin

As I see it every day you do one of two things: build health or produce disease in yourself.
—Adelle Davis

Some folks have more temptations than others because they are always hunting for them.
—Elbert Hubbard

The church is looking for better methods; God is looking for better men.
—E. M. Bounds

It is better to be alone than in bad company.
—George Washington

The things we are going through are either making us sweeter, better and more nobler men and women, or they are making us more critical and fault-finding and more insistent on our own way. The things that happen either make us evil, or they make us more saintly depending entirely on our relationship with God and its level of intimacy.
—Oswald Chambers

People do not seem to realize that their opinion of the world is also a confession of their character.
—Ralph Waldo Emerson

No man can climb out beyond the limitations of his own character.
—John Morley

Character is like a tree and reputation like a shadow. The shadow is what we think of it; the tree is the real thing.
—Abraham Lincoln

Character cannot be developed in ease and quiet. Only through experience of trial and suffering can the soul be strengthened, ambition inspired, and success achieved.
—Helen Keller

Youth is a gift of nature, but age is a work of art.
—Stanislaw Jerzy Lec

The older you get, the more like yourself you become.
—Calvin Thielman

Circumstances don't make the man, they reveal him to himself.
—Epictetus

Crises always reveal a person's true character.
—Oswald Chambers

People are often unreasonable and self-centered. Forgive them anyway. If you are kind, people may accuse you of ulterior motives. Be kind anyway. If you are honest, people may cheat you. Be honest anyway. If you find happiness, people may be jealous. Be happy anyway. The good you do today may be forgotten tomorrow. Do good anyway. Give the world the best you have and it may never be enough. Give your best anyway.
—Mother Teresa

People grow through experience if they meet life honestly and courageously. This is how character is built.
—Eleanor Roosevelt

Before you vote, ask yourself this question, 'Are you a consumer or a producer?'
—John M. Mooney

In character, in manner, in style, in all things, the supreme excellence is simplicity.
—Henry Wadsworth Longfellow

People may doubt what you say, but they will believe what you do.
—Lewis Cass

Where there is no shame, there is no honor.
—African Proverb

Of all properties which belong to honorable men, not one is so highly prized as that of character.
—Henry Clay

No man becomes rich unless he enriches others.
—Andrew Carnegie

Money will only make you more of what you already are.
—T. Harv Eker

The best index to a person's character is how he treats people who can't do him any good, and how he treats people who can't fight back.
—Abigail Van Buren

Character—the willingness to accept responsibility for one's own life—is the source from which self-respect springs.
—Joan Didion

Character is both developed and revealed by tests, and all of life is a test.
—Rick Warren

COMFORT

Answer me when I call, O God of my righteous-
ness! You have given me relief when I was in
distress. Be gracious to me and hear my prayer.
—Psalm 4:1 NIV

I look on all the world as my parish...to declare
unto all that are willing to hear, the glad tidings
of salvation.
—John Wesley

Whenever a pastor is tempted to soft-peddle his
preaching, he should ask, 'What would Jesus do?'
—Klemet I. Preus

You see, if you put a lighted candle in a clay pot, it is
only when it's broken that the light is exposed!
—Frances Young

Now, God be praised, that to believing souls gives
light in darkness, comfort in despair.
—William Shakespeare

Try to be like the turtle—at ease in your own
shell.
—Bill Copeland

Comfort and prosperity have never enriched the world as much as adversity has.
—Billy Graham

Growth and comfort do not coexist.
—Ginni Rometty

Too often we...enjoy the comfort of opinion without the discomfort of thought.
—John F. Kennedy

We find comfort among those who agree with us—growth among those who don't.
—Frank A. Clark

The ultimate measure of a man is not where he stands in moments of comfort and convenience, but where he stands at times of challenge and controversy.
—Martin Luther King Jr.

When someone is crying, of course, the noble thing to do is to comfort them. But if someone is trying to hide their tears, it may also be noble to pretend you do not notice them.
—Lemony Snicket

When life on earth is ending, people don't surround themselves with objects. What we want around us is people—people we love and have relationships with.
—Rick Warren

COMMITMENT

Commit thy way unto the Lord; trust also in Him; and He shall bring it to pass.

—Psalm 37:5 KJB

The kamikaze pilot that was able to fly fifty missions was involved, but never committed.

—Lou Holtz

If you don't design your own life plan, chances are you'll fall into someone else's plan. And guess what they have planned for you? Not much.

—Jim Rohn

Your talent is God's gift to you. What you do with it is your gift back to God.

—Leo Buscaglia

Are we more devoted to service than to Jesus Christ?

—Oswald Chambers

The gospel is not about our ability to think of Christ, but about His promise as the friend of sinners, His promise that nothing will pluck us from His hand.

—Bo Giertz

Anxiety is the natural result when our lives are centered on anything short of God and His will for us
—Billy Graham

Commitment and creativity cannot be captured and handcuffed. Inspiration cannot be jailed. The heart cannot be contained.
—Gary Zukav

Ages of experience have taught humanity that the commitment of a husband and wife to love and to serve one another promotes the welfare of children and the stability of society.
—Jack Kingston

We don't have much to say about how we look at sixteen, but we are the ones who determine how we look at sixty. Examples: exercise, food, stress and fear.
—John M. Mooney

Once you have commitment, you need the discipline and hard work to get you there.
—Haile Gebrselassie

The quality of a man's life is in direct proportion to his commitment to excellence.
—Tom Landry

You were not put on this earth to be remembered, you were put here to prepare for eternity.
—Rick Warren

You become what you think about most of the time.
                              —Brian Tracy

It's not where you start, but where you finish that counts.
                              —Zig Ziglar

Make each day your masterpiece.
                              —John Wooden

The only limit to your impact is your imagination and commitment.
                              —Tony Robbins

You always have two choices: your commitment versus your fear.
                              —Sammy Davis Jr.

Whatever you do, work at it with all your heart, as if working for the Lord, not for human masters.
                              —Colossians 3:23 NIV

Too many Christians have a commitment of convenience. They'll stay faithful as long as it's safe and doesn't involve risk, rejection or criticism. Instead of standing alone in the face of challenge or temptation, they check to see which way their friends are going.
                              —Charles Stanley

I hoped God would be neutral.
                              —Darrell Royal

A Great Commitment to the Great Commandment and the Great Commission will grow a Great Church.

—Rick Warren

And I give them eternal life, and they will never perish, and no one shall snatch them out of My hand.

—John 10:28 ESV

A saint is never consciously a saint; a saint is consciously dependent upon God.

—Oswald Chambers

Sometimes, making the wrong choice is better than making no choice.

—Terry Goodkind

A professional is someone who can do his best work when he doesn't feel like it.

—Alistair Cooke

Man can either drive himself or be driven by someone, but motivation is the key that makes the difference.

—Ronald Mensah

Most people spend more time planning their summer vacation than planning their lives.

—John C. Maxwell

It ought to be the business of every day to prepare for our final day.

—Matthew Henry

COMPASSION

The Lord is merciful and compassionate, slow to get angry and filled with unfailing love.
—Psalm 145:8 NLT

Every day I see Jesus Christ in all of his distressing disguises.
—Mother Teresa

We didn't all come over on the same ship, but today we are all in the same boat.
—Bernard Baruch

Remember, people are different through faulty wiring, DNA, poor programming, parents or mentoring.
—John M. Mooney

Compassion will cure more sins than condemnation.
—Henry Ward Beecher

The heart is the savior of the world, heads do not save.
—E. M. Bounds

Compassion is the basis of morality.
—Arthur Schopenhauer

God's dream is that you and I and all of us will realize that we are family, that we are made for togetherness, for goodness, and for compassion.
—Desmond Tutu

The only time you look into your neighbor's bowl is to make sure they have enough. You don't look into your neighbor's bowl to see if you have as much as them.
—Louis C. K.

Be more concerned with making others feel good about themselves than making them feel good about you.
—Dan Reiland

Love and compassion are necessities, not luxuries. Without them, humanity cannot survive.
—Dalai Lama

I have just three things to teach: simplicity, patience, compassion. These three are your greatest treasures.
—Lao Tzu

Our task must be to free ourselves by widening our circle of compassion to embrace all living creatures and the whole of nature and its beauty.
—Albert Einstein

Until he extends the circle of his compassion to all living things, man will not himself find peace.
—Albert Schweitzer

Courage

They will have no fear of bad news; their hearts are steadfast, trusting in the Lord.
—Psalm 112:7 NIV

Courage is resistance to fear, mastery of fear, not absence of fear.
—Mark Twain

Fake it until you make it, act as if.
—Brian Tracy

Success is not final; failure is not fatal; it is the courage to continue that counts.
—Winston Churchill

Life is supposed to be difficult! It's what enables us to grow.
—Rick Warren

Lord grant me the strength to accept the things I cannot change, the courage to change the things I can, and the wisdom to know the difference.
—Reinhold Niebuhr

Sometimes even to live is an act of courage.
—Lucius Annaeus Seneca

God demands of the sick person nothing other than thanksgiving and endurance.
　　　　　　　　　—St. John Cassian

Courage doesn't always roar. Sometimes courage is the little voice at the end of the day that says I'll try again tomorrow.
　　　　　　　　　—Mary Anne Radmacher

The only tyrant I accept in this world is the still small voice within me. And even though I have to face the prospect of being a minority of one, I humbly believe I have the courage to be in such a hopeless minority.
　　　　　　　　　—Mahatma Gandhi

To live in the past and future is easy. To live in the present is like threading a needle.
　　　　　　　　　—Walker Percy

Courage is being scared to death but saddling up anyway.
　　　　　　　　　—John Wayne

Life without risks is not worth living.
　　　　　　　　　—Charles Lindberg

The hero is one who carries your dreams until you can carry them yourself.
　　　　　　　　　—Jim Hasne

The brave may not live forever—but the cautious do not live at all.
　　　　　　　　　—Richard Branson

Courage is what it takes to stand up and speak; courage is also what it takes to sit down and listen.

—Winston Churchill

Real courage is when you know you're licked before you begin, but you begin anyway and see it through no matter what.

—Harper Lee

Only those who will risk going too far can possibly find out how far one can go.

—T. S. Eliot

If the Bible is true and Jesus is the Messiah, would you be willing to know and follow Him regardless of the consequences?

—Jews for Jesus

The only thing necessary for the triumph of evil is for good men to do nothing.

—Edmund Burke

The blood of the martyrs is the seed of the Church.

—Tertullian

Abide hard by the cross and search the mystery of His wounds.

—Charles H. Spurgeon

Death is just a step into eternal life with God.

—William P. Beck

CREATIVITY

Create in me a clean heart, O God; and renew a right spirit within me.

—Psalm 51:10 KJB

Every child is an artist. The problem is how to remain an artist once we grow up.
—Pablo Picasso

The world is but a canvas to our imagination.
—Henry David Thoreau

Every artist dips his brush in his own soul, and paints his own nature into his pictures.
—Henry Ward Beecher

Creative people are curious, flexible, persistent, and independent with a tremendous spirit of adventure and a love of play.
—Henri Matisse

Develop imagination. Throw away routine.
—Harry Selfridge

To live a creative life, we must lose our fear of being wrong.

—Joseph Chilton Pearce

Originality is nothing but judicious imitation.
—Voltaire

For art to exist, for any sort of aesthetic activity or perception to exist, a certain physiological precondition is indispensable: intoxication.
—Friedrich Nietzsche

Creativity is just connecting things. When you ask creative people how they did something, they feel a little guilty because they really didn't do it, they just saw something. It seemed obvious to them after a while.
—Steve Jobs

The secret to creativity is knowing how to hide your sources.
—Albert Einstein

Creativity is putting your imagination to work, and it's produced the most extraordinary results in human culture.
—Ken Robinson

All great deeds and all great thoughts have a ridiculous beginning.
—Albert Camus

We have to continually be jumping off cliffs and developing our wings on the way down.
—Kurt Vonnegut

EDUCATION

I will instruct you and show you the way to go:
with My eye on you, I will give counsel.
                                        —Psalm 32:8 HCSB

Education is the passport to the future, for tomor-
row belongs to those who prepare for it today.

                                        —Malcolm X

Give a man a fish and you feed him for a day;
teach a man to fish and you feed him for a life-
time.
                                        —Maimonides

A child miseducated is a child lost.
                                        —John F. Kennedy

Education is the ability to listen to almost any-
thing without losing your temper or your self-
confidence.
                                        —Robert Frost

Learning starts with failure; the first failure is the
beginning of education.
                                        —John Hersey

The problem with popular thinking is it does not require any thinking at all.
—Kevin Myers

A short pencil is better than a long memory.
—Unknown

Only the educated are free.
—Epictetus

Learn from the past, prepare for the future, and live in the present.
—Thomas S. Monson

Those who do not learn from history are doomed to repeat it.
—George Santayana

Tell me and I will forget, show me and I may remember, but involve me and I will understand.
—Chinese Proverb

What is the hardest task in the world? 'To think.'
—Ralph Waldo Emerson

Rich people have small TVs and big libraries, and poor people have small libraries and big TVs.

—Zig Ziglar

If a man empties his purse into his head, no man can take it away from him.
—Benjamin Franklin

Education's purpose is to replace an empty mind with an open one.
> —Malcolm Forbes

Education is not preparation of life; education is life itself.
> —John Dewey

Learning is not compulsory...neither is survival.
> —W. Edwards Deming

Each person we meet has the potential to teach us something.
> —John C. Maxwell

It is the mark of an educated mind to be able to entertain a thought without accepting it.
> —Aristotle

I cannot live without books.
> —Thomas Jefferson

The philosophy of the school room in one generation will be the philosophy of government in the next.
> —Abraham Lincoln

Education is the most powerful weapon which you can use to change the world.
> —Nelson Mandela

The direction in which education starts a man will determine his future in life.
> —Plato

FAITH

Trust in the Lord. Have faith, do not despair.
—Psalm 27:14 GNT

For we live by faith, not by sight.
—2 Corinthians 5:7 NIV

Good theology is when God has done his part and Jesus Christ has done your part.
—Klemet I. Preus

It is therefore faith alone which justifies, and yet the faith which justifies is not alone.
—John Calvin

The apostle Peter, an eyewitness to hundreds of Jesus' miracles, nevertheless elevates prophecy over signs and wonders, even over eyewitness accounts.
—Chuck Missler/
Mark Eastman

A state of mind that sees God is evidence of growth in grace and a thankful heart.
—Charles Finney

The Holy Spirit is given to crowd out self.
—John M. Mooney

Keep your faith to the sunshine and you cannot see a shadow. It's what the sunflowers do.
—Helen Keller

Keep close to nature's heart...and break away once in a while and climb a mountain or spend a week in the woods. Wash your spirit clean.
—John Muir

Faith sees the invisible, believes the unbelievable and receives the impossible.
—Corrie ten Boom

Faith is taking the first step even when you don't see the whole staircase.
—Martin Luther King Jr.

For the faithful, there are no questions—for the nonbeliever, there are no answers.
—Rabbi Yakor

If you don't feel as close to God today as you did yesterday, who moved?
—Chris Heimerdinger

Faith never knows where it is being led but it knows and loves the One who is leading.
—Oswald Chambers

The just shall live by faith, not by feelings.
—Don Johnson

Faith is the gaze of the soul upon a saving God.
—A. W. Tozer

For as the body without the spirit is dead, so faith without works is dead also.
—James 2:26 NASB

The best reply to an atheist is to give him a great dinner and ask if he believes there is a cook.
—Louis Nizer

Jesus said to him, 'Have you believed because you have seen Me? Blessed are those who have not seen, and yet have believed.
—John 20:29 ESV

Doubt is merely the seed of faith; a sign that faith is alive and ready to grow.
—Kathleen Norris

I had rather experience faith than know the definition thereof.
—A. W. Tozer

The church is composed of equal parts mystery and mess.
—Eugene H. Peterson

Going to church doesn't make you a Christian any more than standing in a garage makes you a car.
—Billy Sunday

The one most important thing in life is our attitude toward God. Everything depends on that.
—Henry H. Halley

God's delays are not God's denials.
—Robert H. Schuller

It is possible to know all doctrine and yet not know Jesus. The soul is in danger when knowledge of doctrine outsteps intimate touch with Jesus.
—Oswald Chambers

For I can testify about them that they are zealous for God, but their zeal is not based on knowledge.
—Romans 10:2 NIV

Those who have the disease called Jesus will never be cured.
—Brennan Manning

The faith by which we are justified is faith. Faith is like a channel, through which the benefits of Christ flow to us.
—Alister McGrath

Many people begin to come to Jesus Christ once they stop being religious.
—John M. Mooney

Eternal life does not begin with death, it begins with faith.
—Samuel Shoemaker

Faith in oneself is the best and safest course.
—Michelangelo

Satan does not come along the line of tempting us to sin, but on the line of shifting the point of view to God.

—Oswald Chambers

You contribute nothing to salvation except the sin that made it necessary.

—Jonathan Edwards

Faith doesn't get you around trouble, problems in life and relationships, it gets you through it.
—Jonathon Anthony Burkett

True faith is not about trying; rather it's about dying in Christ.

—Watchman Nee

So then, those who are of faith are blessed along with Abraham, the man of faith.
—Galatians 3:9 ESV

Faith is to believe what you do not see; the reward of this faith is to see what you believe.
—St. Augustine

Faith has to do with things that are not seen and hope with things that are not at hand.
—Thomas Aquinas

No dependence will I have upon my prayings, my doings, my feelings...simply to thy Cross I cling.
—Charles H. Spurgeon

There are many things that are essential to arriving at true peace of mind, and one of the most important is faith, which cannot be acquired without prayer.

—John Wooden

To have faith is to trust yourself to the water. When you swim you don't grab hold of the water, because if you do you will sink and drown. Instead you relax and float.

—Alan Watts

Faith is the bird that feels the light and sings when the dawn is still dark.

—Rabindranath Tagore

Faithless is he that says farewell when the road darkens.

—J. R. R. Tolkien

Faith is the oasis that will never be reached by the caravan of thinking.

—Kahlil Gibran

Be faithful in small things because it is in them that your strength lies.

—Mother Teresa

A man of courage is also full of faith.

—Marcus Tullius Cicero

Faith is not belief without proof, but trust without reservation.

—D. Elton Trueblood

FEAR

Even when I walk through the valley of the shadow of death, I will fear no evil, for You are with me; Your rod and Your staff, they comfort me.
—Psalm 23:4 ESV

It is hard to fail, but it is worse never to have tried to succeed.
—Theodore Roosevelt

Fear kills more people than death.
—General George Patton

All the water of the seven seas cannot sink a single ship unless it gets inside the ship.
—Goi Nasu

The person who risks nothing, does nothing, has nothing, is nothing and becomes nothing.
—Leo Buscaglia

He who is not everyday conquering some fear has not learned the secret of life.
—Ralph Waldo Emerson

Fear is excitement without breath.
—Robert Hiller

Our doubts are our traitors.
—William Shakespeare

People are never more insecure than when they become obsessed with their fears at the expense of their dreams.
—Norman Cousins

When you get rid of your fear of failure, your tensions about succeeding...you can be yourself. You'll no longer be driving with your brakes on.
—Anthony de Mello

Fear of man will prove to be a snare, but whoever trusts in the Lord is kept safe.
—Proverbs 29:25 NIV

Many people are driven by guilt, resentment, anger, fear, materialism or approval.
—Rick Warren

Fear is the greatest obstacle to learning, but fear is your best friend.
—Mike Tyson

'Fear not' is the most repeated command in the Bible.
—Bill Gaultiere

People who have no fear of God soon have no fear of man—no respect for human laws and authorities.
—Charles Colson

We can easily forgive a child who is afraid of the dark; the real tragedy of life is when men are afraid of the light.

—Plato

I was never afraid of failure, for I would sooner fail than not be among the best.

—John Keats

Everything you want is on the other side of fear.

—Jack Canfield

The oldest and strongest emotion of mankind is fear, and the oldest and strongest kind of fear is fear of the unknown.

—H. P. Lovecraft

Do one thing every day that scares you.

—Eleanor Roosevelt

Go back a little to leap further.

—John Clark

There is no such thing as paranoia. Your worst fears can come true at any moment.

—Hunter S. Thompson

Nothing in life is to be feared. It is only to be understood. Now is the time to understand more, so that we may fear less.

—Marie Curie

It is easy to be brave from a distance.

—Aesop

FORESIGHT

I lift up my eyes to the hills. From where will my help come? My help comes from the Lord, Who made heaven and earth.

—Psalm 121:1-2 ESV

Among all My creatures, only humans can anticipate future events.

—Sarah Young

A person starts to live when he can live outside of himself.

—Albert Einstein

Think from the end.

—Wayne W. Dyer

I'm cursed with the gift of foresight.

—Steven P. Morrissey

Fear is the mother of foresight.

—Thomas Hardy

Whatever you think about most of your time grows and increases in your life.

—Brian Tracy

Every word has consequences. Every silence too.

—Jean-Paul Sartre

For the word of God is alive and active. Sharper than any double-edged sword, it penetrates even to dividing soul and spirit, joints and marrow; it judges the thoughts and attitudes of the heart.
—Hebrews 4:12 NIV

Choose your friends carefully. Your enemies will choose you.
—Yassir Arafat

It is pardonable to be defeated, but never to be surprised.
—Frederick the Great

A leader who doesn't hesitate before he sends his nation into battle is not fit to be a leader.
—Golda Meir

Forethought we may have, undoubtedly, but not foresight.
—Napoléon Bonaparte

In the land of the blind, the one-eyed man is king.

—Desiderius Erasmus

Prudence is foresight and farsightedness. It's the ability to make immediate decisions on the basis of their longer-range effects.
—John Ortberg

Planning for tomorrow is time well spent, worrying about tomorrow is time wasted.
—Neil S. Wilson

A budget is people telling their money where to go instead of wondering where it went.
—Dave Ramsey

Thrift comes too late when you find it at the bottom of your purse.
—Lucius Anneaus Seneca

Sometimes your best investments are the ones you don't make.
—Donald Trump

You hire for skill and fire for attitude. Your attitude, not your aptitude, will determine your altitude.
—Richard Crooks

If you only look at what is, you might never attain what could be.
—Anonymous

No matter what happens, there's always somebody who knew it would.
—Lonny Starr

You cannot make progress without making decisions.
—Jim Rohn

No matter how many mistakes you make or how slow your progress, you're still way ahead of everyone who isn't trying.
—Tony Robbins

FORGIVENESS

He continues to forgive all your sins; He continues to heal all your diseases.

—Psalm 103:3 ISV

To understand all is to forgive all.
—Madame de Staël

Forgive all who have offended you. Not for them, but for yourself.

—Harriet Nelson

He that cannot forgive others, breaks the bridge over which he must pass himself; for every man has need to be forgiven.
—Thomas Fuller

You forgive mistakes; you punish patterns.
—Jonah Goldberg

Forgotten is forgiven.

—F. Scott Fitzgerald

The forgiveness of real wrongs is always a form of suffering.

—Dietrich Bonhoeffer

And so I tell you, every kind of sin and slander can be forgiven, but blasphemy against the spirit will not be forgiven.
—Matthew 12:31 NIV

Every twenty-four hours God has a fresh new supply of grace, of favor, of wisdom, of forgiveness.
—Joel Osteen

In this life our suffering is never as great or serious as our sin.
—C. J. Mahaney

God delivers us from sin—we have to deliver ourselves from our individuality.
—Oswald Chambers

To forgive is to set a prisoner free and discover that the prisoner was you.
—Lewis B. Smedes

Those you hate control your future.
—John M. Mooney

We must develop and maintain the capacity to forgive. He who is devoid of the power to forgive is devoid of the power to love. There is some good in the worst of us and some evil in the best of us.
—Martin Luther King Jr.

The weak can never forgive. Forgiveness is the attribute of the strong.
—Mahatma Gandhi

Life becomes easier when you learn to accept an apology you never got.
> —Robert Brault

Mistakes are always forgivable, if one has the courage to admit to them.
> —Bruce Lee

Everyone who forgives someone bears the other's sins.
> —Dietrich Bonhoeffer

God can forgive your sins, but your body may not.
> —John M. Mooney

Repentance means you change your mind so deeply it changes you.
> —Bruce Wilkinson

Don't wait to forgive until you feel like forgiving; you will never get there. Feelings take time to heal after the choice to forgive is made.
> —Neil T. Anderson

I am the living bread that came down from heaven. Whoever eats this bread will live forever. This bread is My flesh, which I will give for the life of the world.
> —John 6:51 NIV

Forgiveness is the final form of love.
> —Reinhold Niebuhr

GENEROSITY

Good will comes to those who are generous and lend freely, who conduct their affairs with justice.

—Psalm 112:5 NIV

God does not need our good works, but your neighbor does.
—Martin Luther

Always give without remembering and always receive without forgetting.
—Brian Tracy

Only a life lived for others is a life worthwhile.
—Albert Einstein

The purest form of love is given with no expectations of return.
—David Hubbard

Generosity is the flower of justice.
—Nathaniel Hawthorne

The poor don't know that their function in life is to exercise our generosity.
—Jean-Paul Sartre

God's children worry and help His other children. Satan's children claim their right to self.
—John M. Mooney

I'm a disciple of Jesus Christ and I serve Him by serving you, since that's what He came to do.
—Doug Weible

You give but little when you give of your possessions. It is when you give of yourself that you truly give.
—Kahlil Gibran

The hero is the man that forgets himself for others.
—René Quinton

You cannot live a perfect day without doing something for someone who will never be able to repay you.
—John Wooden

We make a living by what we get, but we make a life by what we give.
—Winston Churchill

Gentleness, self-sacrifice and generosity are the exclusive possession of no one race or religion.
—Mahatma Gandhi

The entire population of the world—with one minor exception—is composed of others.
—John C. Maxwell

Complete possession is proved only by giving. All you are unable to give possesses you.
—André Gide

The practice of secrecy is Jesus' gift to approval addicts.
—John Ortberg

Leadership is learning to give whether or not you get anything. If you ever give to get something, you're not giving; you're trading.
—Charles Tremendous Jones

Let us try to teach generosity and altruism, because we are born selfish.
—Richard Dawkins

Real generosity is doing something nice for someone who will never find out.
—Frank A. Clark

Real generosity toward the future lies in giving all to the present.
—Albert Camus

Generosity has built America. When we fail to invest in children, we have to pay the cost.
—Bob Keeshan

The best use of life is to spend it for something that will outlast it.
—William James

Goals

*But the plans of the Lord stand firm forever, the
purpose of His heart all through generations.*
—Psalm 33:11 NIV

*Give me a stock clerk with a goal and I'll give you
a man who will make history. Give me a man
with no goals and I'll give you a stock clerk.*
—J. C. Penney

*Obstacles are those frightful things you see when
you take your eyes off the goals.*
—Henry Ford

Our intention creates our reality.
—Wayne W. Dyer

*Nothing can add more power to your life than
concentrating all your energies on a limited set of
targets.*
—Nido Qubein

*Gather in your resources, rally all your faculties,
marshal all your energies, focus all your capaci-
ties upon mastery of at least one field of endeavor.*
—John Hagee

Setting goals is the first step in turning the invisible into the visible.
—Tony Robbins

Discipline is the bridge between goals and accomplishments.
—Jim Rohn

Nothing can stop the man with the right mental attitude from achieving his goal; nothing on earth can help the man with the wrong mental attitude.
—Thomas Jefferson

If you want to run fast, run alone. If you want to run far, run together.
—African Proverb

If you can imagine it, you can achieve it. If you can dream it, you can become it.
—William Arthur Ward

A goal without a plan is just a wish.
—Antoine de Saint-Exupéry

Only three percent of adults have written goals, everyone else works for them.
—Brian Tracy

If you want to live a happy life, tie it to a goal, not to people or things.
—Albert Einstein

GOODNESS

*They celebrate Your abundant goodness and joy-
fully sing of Your righteousness.*
—Psalm 145:7 NIV

*A heart is not judged by how much you love, but
by how much you are loved by others.*
—L. Frank Baum

*A saint is not someone who is good but who expe-
riences the goodness of God.*
—Brennan Manning

*The measure of life is not its duration, but its
donation.*
—Peter Marshall

Evil is always possible. Goodness is a difficulty.
—Anne Rice

Good has always been more deceptive than evil.

—Rick Joyner

*Believing the best in people usually brings the best
out of people.*
—John C. Maxwell

Each of us sees in others what we carry in our own hearts.

—Ralph Waldo Emerson

Don't let evil conquer you, but conquer evil by doing good.

—Romans 12:21 NLT

Confidence in the goodness of another is good proof of one's own goodness.

—Michel de Montaigne

Man has two spiritual needs. One is for forgiveness. The other is for goodness.

—Billy Graham

And if I say again that the greatest good of man is daily to converse about virtue, and all that concerning which you hear me examining myself and others, and that the life which is unexamined is not worth living.

—Socrates

Goodness is the only investment that never fails.

—Henry David Thoreau

The fragrance of flowers spreads only in the direction of the wind. But the goodness of a person spreads in all directions.

—Chanakya

It is good people who make good places.

—Anna Sewell

We look to God to exhibit himself to His children, but God only exhibits Himself in His children.
—Oswald Chambers

Good relations with God the Father depends on good relations with His children.
—John M. Mooney

The greatest need of my people is my personal holiness.
—Robert Murray
M'Cheyne

No one can be good for long if goodness is not in demand.
—Bertolt Brecht

You should also appreciate the goodness around you, and surround yourself with positive people.
—Nadia Comaneci

Let you look for the goodness in me, and judge me not.
—Arthur Miller

The roots of all goodness lie in the soil of appreciation for goodness.
—Dalai Lama

Virtue is bold, and goodness never fearful.
— William Shakespeare

How we treat others will be our epitaphs.
— Jon Huntsman

GRACE

Give ear, O Lord, to my prayer; listen to my plea for grace.

—Psalm 86:6 ESV

Man is born broken. He lives by mending. The grace of God is glue.

—Eugene O'Neill

Grace, like water, always flows downward, to the lowest place.

—Philip Yancey

Rain is grace; rain is the sky descending on the earth; without rain, there would be no life.

—John Updike

There is no pit so deep that God's love is not deeper still.

—Corrie ten Boom

The gospel of grace announces: God's forgiveness precedes repentance.

—Brennan Manning

Above all grace and the gifts that Christ gives to His beloved is that of overcoming self.

—St. Francis of Assisi

All the natural movements of the soul are controlled by laws analogous to those of physical gravity. Grace is the only exception. Grace fills empty spaces, but it can only enter where there is a void to receive it, and it is grace itself which makes this void. The imagination is continually at work filling up all the fissures through which grace might pass.
—Simone Weil

True spirituality consists in living moment by moment by the grace of Jesus Christ.
—Francis Shaeffer

The world can do almost anything as well or better than the church. You need not be a Christian to build houses, feed the hungry, or heal the sick. There is only one thing the world cannot do. It cannot offer grace.
—Gordon McDonald

Sin does not stop God's grace from flowing, but God's grace will stop sin.
—Joseph Prince

Courage is grace under pressure.
—Ernest Hemmingway

Grace offers rest. Legalism never does.
—Max Lucado

For me, every hour is grace.
—Elie Wiesel

We go to a higher level when we treat others better than the way they treat us.
—John C. Maxwell

Learn to...be what you are, and learn to resign with good grace all that you are not.
—Henri Frédéric Amiel

The ideal man bears the accidents of life with dignity and grace, making the best of circumstances.
—Aristotle

God took a risk by announcing forgiveness in advance, and the scandal of grace involves a transfer of that risk to us.
—Philip Yancey

I am only one, but I am one. I can't do everything, but I can do something. The something I ought to do, I can do. And by the grace of God I will do.
—Edward Everett Hale

The perfection of Christian character depends wholly upon the grace and strength found alone in God.
—Ellen G. White

Jesus wept. Voltaire smiled. From that divine tear and from that human smile is derived the grace of current civilization.
—Victor Hugo

GRATITUDE

This is the day the Lord has made. We will rejoice and be glad in it.

—Psalm 118:24 NLT

Rarely do we get everything we want and I imagine the same holds true for God.

—Philip Yancey

Develop a grateful heart. Eliminate your sense of entitlement.

—Steven K. Scott

It's not whether the glass is half full or half empty; it's who is pouring the water.

—Mark Cuban

Now is the winter of our discontent.

—William Shakespeare

Before you fall asleep at night, meditate about being faithful, grateful and spiritual; don't dwell on the self.

—John M. Mooney

If you don't think every day is a good day, just try skipping one.

—Cavett Robert

When we choose not to focus on what is missing from our lives but are grateful for the abundance that's present...we experience heaven on earth.
— Sara Ban Breathnach

Develop an attitude of gratitude, and give thanks for everything that happens to you, knowing that every step forward is a step toward achieving something bigger and better than your current situation.
— Brian Tracy

Feeling gratitude and not expressing it is like wrapping a present and not giving it.
— William Arthur Ward

Joy is the simplest form of gratitude.
— Karl L. Barth

Among the things you can give and still keep are your word, a smile, and a grateful heart.
— Zig Ziglar

When a person doesn't have gratitude, something is missing in his humanity.
— Elie Wiesel

As we express our gratitude, we must never forget that the highest appreciation is not to utter words, but to live by them.
— John F. Kennedy

Gratitude is the sign of noble souls.
— Aesop

HAPPINESS

Hallelujah! Happy is the person who fears the Lord, taking great delight in His commands.
—Psalm 112:1 HCSB

If you want to be happy, be.
—Leo Tolstoy

I don't sing because I'm happy; I'm happy because I sing.
—William James

No one on his deathbed ever said, 'I wish I had spent more time on my business.'
—Paul Tsongas

You must choose between your attachment and happiness. You cannot have both.
—Anthony de Mello

There is no way to happiness—happiness is the way.
—Thich Nhat Hanh

Some pursue happiness—others create it.
—Ralph Waldo Emerson

No one knows enough to be a pessimist.
—Norman Cousins

The true test of relationships is not how loyal we are when friends fail, but how thrilled we are when they succeed.

—John C. Maxwell

You cannot hang out with negative people and expect to live a positive life.

—Joel Osteen

To be happy at home is the ultimate result of all ambition.

—Samuel Johnson

Happiness is not a matter of intensity but of balance, order, rhythm and harmony.

—Thomas Merton

He who has health, has hope; and he who has hope, has everything.

—Thomas Carlyle

There is only one happiness in this life, to love and be loved.

—George Sand

Be happy for this moment. This moment is your life.

—Omar Khayyam

Happiness cannot be traveled to, owned, earned, worn or consumed. Happiness is the spiritual experience of living every moment with love, grace and gratitude.

—Denis Waitley

HEALING

He sent out His word and healed them; snatching them from the door of death.

—Psalm 107:20 NLT

The soul is healed by being with children.
—Fyodor Dostoevsky

I'm a little pencil in the hand of a writing God, who is sending a love letter to the world.
—Mother Teresa

Simple kindness to one's self and all that lives is the most powerful transformational force of all.
—David R. Hawkins

Understanding God's use of illness and how its ultimate purpose is to prosper the soul brings great insight.
—Jean-Claude Larchet

AEDS: Acquired Evil Disposition Syndrome.
—Emmanuel Hatzidakis

Take care of your body. It's the only place you have to live.
—Jim Rohn

Earth has no sorrow that Heaven cannot heal.
—David Crowder

The church is a hospital for sinners, not a museum for saints.
—Abigail Van Buren

In fact, any Pharisee could have made a fool out of Mary doctrinally, but one thing they could never ridicule was the fact that Jesus had cast seven demons out of her.
—Oswald Chambers

God comforts us to make us comforters, not to make us comfortable.
—Ray C. Stedman

And Jesus said to him, 'Go. Your faith has healed you.' Instantly the man could see, and he followed Jesus down the road.
—Mark 10:52 NLT

Healing is a matter of time, but it is sometimes also a matter of opportunity.
—Hippocrates

The art of healing comes from nature, not from the physician. Therefore the physician must start from nature, with an open mind.
—Paracelsus

The wilderness is healing, a therapy for the soul.
—Nicholas Kristof

HONESTY

*But You desire honesty from the womb, teaching
me wisdom from there.*

—Psalm 51:6 NLT

*If you find yourself in a hole, the first thing you
should do is stop digging.*

—Will Rogers

Honesty is never seen sitting astride the fence.

—Lemuel K. Washburn

*Criticism is something that you can avoid easily
by saying nothing and becoming nothing.*

—Aristotle

It is better to offer no excuse than a bad one.

—George Washington

*Being entirely honest with oneself is a good exer-
cise.*

—Sigmund Freud

Who I am is what I see.

—Noel Coward

Are you Christ-centered or self-centered?

—Terry Hardy Olsen

How desperately difficult it is to be honest with oneself. It is much easier to be honest with other people.
—Edward Benson

We tend to become what we degrade.
—Jon Huntsman

If you really want to understand a man, don't just listen to what he says but watch what he does.
—Maurice Blondel

Honesty is the fastest way to prevent a mistake from turning into a failure.
—James Altucher

Honesty prospers in every condition of life.
—Friedrich Schiller

Promise only what you can deliver and then deliver more than what you promise.
—Unknown

Have you realized most of your unhappiness in life is due to the fact that you are listening to yourself instead of talking to yourself?
—Martyn Lloyd-Jones

Every man should keep a fair-sized cemetery in which to bury the faults of his friends.
—Henry Ward Beecher

No legacy is a so rich as honesty.
—William Shakespeare

HUMILITY

The Lord lifts up the humble; He casts the wicked to the ground.

—Psalm 147:6 ESV

Don't be so humble, you're not that great.
—Golda Meir

Humility is the oil that smooths and soothes relationships.

—Rick Warren

True humility is contentment.
—Henri Frédéric Amiel

Can you imagine a life in which you refuse to enjoy a single word of approval, appreciation or to lean on someone's arm?
—Anthony de Mello

Humility means the better you know God, the less you have to prove.

—Doug Britton

Humility is to make a right estimate of oneself.
—Charles H. Spurgeon

Humility is truth.

—Desiderius Erasmus

The basic human problem is that everyone believes there is a God and I am it.
—Philip Yancey

In himself nothing, in God everything.
—A. W. Tozer

You must hide under the veil of humility, transferring with joy all the glory you possess to God your Father.
—Timothy J. Keller

Paul always attracted people to Jesus, never to himself.
—Oswald Chambers

To be humble means you are teachable.
—Michael Taylor

It is only through the opposition of ideas that we can learn to be self-critical, to work towards intellectual humility.
—Tariq Ramadan

True humility is to let good be done through me without my being aware of it.
—Mother Teresa

Only in death of the ego is there true freedom, peace, serenity and joy.
—Anonymous

It ain't the heat, it's the humility.
—Yogi Berra

We must go to God as a child, because only a child gets his prayers answered; a 'wise' man does not.
—Oswald Chambers

It was pride that changed angels into devils; it is humility that makes men as angels.
—St. Augustine

Praise in public, criticize in private.
—Vince Lombardi

Pride is concerned with who is right. Humility is concerned with what is right.
—Ezra Taft Benson

Humility is not thinking less of yourself, it's thinking of yourself less.
—C. S. Lewis

When you win, say nothing, and when you lose, say less. —Paul Brown

Early in life I had to choose between honest arrogance and hypocritical humility. I chose the former and have seen no reason to change.
—Frank Lloyd Wright

Life is a long lesson in humility.
—James M. Barrie

He who dies with the most toys is, nonetheless, still dead.

—Anonymous

INSIGHT

Yes, I have more insight than my teachers, for I am always thinking of your laws.
—Psalm 119:99 NLT

It is a 'greater miracle that a person can see his true self than the raising of the dead.'
—St. Isaac

Listen to the inner voice that is on the other side of your ego.
—Aniello Grimaldi

Knowing others is wisdom, knowing yourself is Enlightenment.
—Lao Tzu

A leader is one who knows the way, goes the way, and shows the way.
—John C. Maxwell

The man with insight enough to admit his limitations comes nearest to perfection.
—Johann Wolfgang
von Goethe

There is a kind of beauty in imperfection.
—Conrad Hall

*What lies behind us and what lies before us are
tiny matters compared to what lies within us.*
—Ralph Waldo Emerson

*Because once you see yourself as the problem, you
can see yourself as the solution.*
—Steve Chandler

*The cause of my irritation is not with this person,
but in me.*
—Anthony de Mello

*It's not what you eat that will kill you as much as
what is eating you.*
—Orrin Woodward

*When Bob has a problem with everyone, Bob is
usually the problem.*
—John C. Maxwell

Do not judge, or you too will be judged.
—Matthew 7:1 NIV

*But 'the Lord is my helper' this very moment,
even in my present circumstances.*
—Oswald Chambers

*In form, you receive in-formation; when you
move to spirit you receive in-spiration.*
—Wayne W. Dyer

Nothing happens unless first a dream.
—Carl Sandberg

We cannot know God without first being aware of ourselves. We cannot accurately know ourselves without first knowing God.
>   —R. C. Sproul

If I am not for myself, who will be for me? If I am only for myself, what am I?...And if not now, when?
>   —Rabbi Hillel

It is not a question of God 'sending us' to Hell. In each of us there is something growing which will of itself be Hell unless it is nipped in the bud.
>   —C. S. Lewis

Everyone is a moon, and has a dark side which he never shows to anybody.
>   —Mark Twain

An optimist may see light where there is none, but why must the pessimist always run to blow it out?
>   —René Descartes

Your thoughts too are vibrations of energy, positive or negative...You cannot think both negative and positive thoughts at the same time.
>   —John Kehoe

Knowing is not understanding. There is a great difference between knowing and understanding: you can know a lot about something and not understand it.
>   —Charles F. Kettering

Our patience will achieve more than our force.
                          —Edmund Burke

*You will not be punished for your anger; you will
be punished by your anger.*
                          —Buddha

*Is it Reality you are responding to or is it your as-
sumptions about it?*
                          —Anthony de Mello

*As a rule what is out of sight disturbs men's minds
more seriously than what they see.*
                          —Julius Caesar

*If you are living in the past or in the future, you
will never find a meaning in the present.*
                          —Fausto Cercignani

*Sin is not simply doing bad things, it is putting
good things in the place of God.*
                          —C. S. Lewis

*It's not only the questions you ask, but the ques-
tions you fail to ask, that shape your destiny.*
                          —Tony Robbins

*If you want to understand today, you have to
search yesterday.*
                          —Pearl Buck

*Understanding human needs is half the job of
meeting them.*
                          —Adlai E. Stevenson

You've got to circulate to percolate.
—Cavett Robert

Emotion is created by motion.
—Anthony Robbins

You are never a great man when you have more mind than heart.
—E. P. Beauchene

Beware of posing as a profound person—God became a baby.
—Oswald Chambers

Every preacher I know says that a man's relationship with his father tremendously impacts his relationship with his Heavenly Father.
—Stephen Arterburn/
Fred Stoeker

We always become like the one we worship.
—Bill Johnson

A sense of urgency is that feeling that lets you know yesterday is gone forever, tomorrow never comes. Today is in your hands.
—Charles Tremendous
Jones

Premature responsibility breeds superficiality.
—Albert Einstein

Youth is wasted on the young.
—George Bernard Shaw

I have frequently gained my first real insight into the character of parents by studying their children.

—Sir Arthur Conan Doyle

What will your legacy be after you close your eyes?

—John M. Mooney

It seems that if one is working from the point of view of getting beauty in one's equations, and if one has really a sound insight, one is on a sure line of progress.

—Paul Dirac

If you understand everything, you must be misinformed.

—Japanese Proverb

Outsiders have an insight that an insider doesn't quite have.

—Diane Abbott

There is nothing so terrible as activity without insight.

—Johann Wolfgang
von Goethe

Humor is the affectionate communication of insight.

—Leo Rosten

The best vision is insight.

—Malcolm Forbes

JOY

Shout to the Lord, all the earth; break out in praise and sing for joy!

—Psalm 98:4 NLT

True joy comes to those who have devoted their lives to something greater than their own personal happiness.

—John Ortberg

Each of us are like angels with only one wing; we can fly only by embracing each other.

—Luciano de Crescenzo

Take yourself lightly if you want to fly.

—G. K. Chesterton

Joy is prayer. Joy is strength. Joy is love. Joy is a net of love by which you can catch souls.

—Mother Teresa

Being free is nothing; becoming free is everything.

—Johann Gottlieb Fichte

Those who bring sunshine to the lives of others cannot keep it from themselves.

—James Matthew Barrie

Service which is rendered without joy helps neither the servant nor the served. But all other pleasures and possessions pale into nothingness before service which is rendered in a spirit of joy.
—Mahatma Gandhi

Grief can take care of itself, but to get the full value of joy, you must have somebody to divide it with.
—Mark Twain

When you enjoy the little things in life, you may look back and realize they were the big things.
—Kurt Vonnegut

Learning to live in the present moment is part of the path of joy.
—Sarah Ban Breathnach

Sometimes your joy is the source of your smile, but sometimes your smile can be the source of your joy.
—Thich Nhat Hanh

Happiness is something that just happens because of the arrangement of circumstances, but joy endures in spite of circumstances.
—John Hunter

We should all do what, in the long run, gives us joy, even if it is only picking grapes or sorting the laundry.
—E. B. White

Worry never robs tomorrow of its sorrow, it only saps today of its joy.
—Leo Buscaglia

Tears of joy are like the summer rain drops pierced by sunbeams.
—Hosea Ballou

Find a place inside where there's joy, and the joy will burn out the pain.
—Joseph Campbell

You must submit to supreme suffering in order to discover the completion of joy.
—John Calvin

Joy's smile is much closer to tears than laughter.
—Victor Hugo

It is a fact that the oldest, saddest people are those who outlived enthusiasm.
—Norman Vincent Peale

Joy is not the absence of suffering, it is the presence of God.
—Robert H. Schuller

Joy is the infallible sign of the presence of God.
—Pierre Teilhard
de Chardin

Joy is the serious business of heaven.
—C. S. Lewis

KINDNESS

*Because Thy loving kindness is better than life, my
lips shall praise Thee.*

> —Psalm 63:3 KJB

*No exercise is better for the human heart than
reaching down and lifting another up.*
> —John Andrew Holmes

*A single act of kindness throws out roots in all
directions, and the roots spring up and make new
trees.*
> —Amelia Earhart

Kindness is always fashionable and welcome.
> —Amelia Barr

*God so identifies with the poor that their cries
express divine pain.*
> —John Calvin

*Do people let you down? Don't carry them on your
shoulders. Take them into your heart.*
> —Dom Hélder Câmara

*Caring for people should proceed confronting
people.*
> —John C. Maxwell

Most emotional illness is due to belittling ourselves and others.
                                        —John M. Mooney

I must be cruel only to be kind. Thus bad begins and worse remains behind.
                                        —William Shakespeare

Kind words can be short and easy to speak, but their echoes are truly endless.
                                        —Mother Teresa

You can accomplish by kindness what you cannot by force.
                                        —Publilius Syrus

If you have a choice between being right or being kind, choose kindness.
                                        —Wayne W. Dyer

Kindness is the language which the deaf can hear and the blind can see.
                                        —Mark Twain

A warm smile is the universal language of kindness.
                                        —William Arthur Ward

Everyone responds to kindness.
                                        —Richard Gere

No act of kindness, no matter how small, is ever wasted.
                                        —Aesop

Be nice to your children. After all, they are going to choose your nursing home.
                    —Steven Wright

The words of the tongue should have three gate-keepers: Is it true? Is it kind? Is it necessary?
                    —Arabic Proverb

Wherever there is a human being, there is an opportunity for kindness.
                    —Lucius Annaeus Seneca

Kindness is more important than wisdom and the recognition of this is the beginning of wisdom.
                    —Theodore Isaac Rubin

You cannot do a kindness too soon for you never know how soon it will be too late.
                    —Ralph Waldo Emerson

If you want to lift yourself up, lift up someone else.
                    —Booker T. Washington

A part of kindness consists in loving people more than they deserve.
                    —Joseph Joubert

My religion is very simple. My religion is kindness.
                    —Dalai Lama

KNOWLEDGE

I believe in Your commands; now teach me good judgment and knowledge.
> —Psalm 119:66 NLT

To be conscious that you are ignorant is a great step to knowledge.
> —Benjamin Disraeli

Real knowledge is to know the extent of one's ignorance.
> —Confucius

Ignorance is the night of the mind.
> —William Shakespeare

More gold has been mined from the thoughts of man than has ever been taken from the earth.
> —Napoleon Hill

The true sign of intelligence is not knowledge but imagination.
> —Albert Einstein

He who asks questions cannot avoid answers.
> —African Proverb

It is the knowledge of God, not the knowledge about God.

—A. W. Tozer

He that has doctrinal knowledge and speculation only, without affection, never is engaged in the business of religion.

—Jonathan Edwards

When you have knowledge, you use a torch to show the way; when you are enlightened, you become a torch.

—Anthony de Mello

The New is in the Old concealed; the Old is the New revealed.

—St. Augustine

A great many people think they are thinking when they are merely rearranging their prejudices.

—William James

What ever we think about and thank about is what we bring about.

—John F. Demartini

All knowledge begins with the senses, proceeds then to the understanding, and ends with reason. There is nothing higher than reason.

—Immanuel Kant

Where there is shouting, there is no true knowledge.

—Leonardo da Vinci

We think too much and feel too little; more than machinery we need humanity.
　　　　　　　　—Charlie Chaplin

The shortest and best ways to make your fortune is to let people see clearly that it is in their best interests to promote yours.
　　　　　　　　—Jean de La Bruyère

There are only four core buying emotions: mad, glad, scared and sad...Every purchase in every market is emotionally motivated.
　　　　　　　　—Dr. Sharon Livingston

Good judgment comes from experience and a lot of that comes from poor judgment.
　　　　　　　　—Will Rogers

You can't solve a problem with the same mind that created it.
　　　　　　　　—Albert Einstein

Every addition to true knowledge is an addition to human power.
　　　　　　　　—Horace Mann

For me, I am driven by two main philosophies: know more today about the world than I knew yesterday and lessen the suffering of others. You'd be surprised how far that gets you.
　　　　　　　　—Neil deGrasse Tyson

Wonder is the desire for knowledge.
　　　　　　　　—St. Thomas Aquinas

And seeing ignorance is the curse of God, Knowledge is the wing wherewith we fly to heaven.
—William Shakespeare

The larger the island of knowledge, the longer the shoreline of wonder.
—Ralph W. Sockman

Knowledge has to be improved, challenged, and increased constantly, or it vanishes.
—Peter Drucker

Knowledge rests not upon truth alone, but upon error also.
—Carl Jung

We are drowning in information, while starving for wisdom.
—E. O. Wilson

We are all born ignorant, but one must work hard to remain stupid.
—Benjamin Franklin

To know that we know what we know, and to know that we do not know what we do not know, that is true knowledge.
—Nicolaus Copernicus

Death always means separation, never extinction, so putting to death the deeds of the body cannot mean eradicating them.
—Charles C. Ryrie

LONELINESS

For my father and mother have forsaken me, but the Lord will take me in.

—Psalm 27:10 ESV

The mass of men lead lives of quiet desperation. What is called resignation is confirmed desperation.

—Henry David Thoreau

What loneliness is more lonely than distrust?
—George Eliot

Loneliness is proof that your innate search for connection is intact.

—Martha Beck

Loneliness is not cured by human company. Loneliness is cured by contact with reality.
—Anthony de Mello

The loneliness you get by the sea is personal and alive. It doesn't subdue you and make you feel abject. It's stimulating loneliness.

—Anne Morrow Lindbergh

Loneliness comes with life.

—Whitney Houston

'Jesus wept' is the shortest and biggest verse in the Bible.

—E. M. Bounds

God often visits us, but most of the time we are not at home.

—Philibert Joseph Roux

All sins are attempts to fill voids.
—Simone Weil

The story goes that a public sinner was excommunicated and forbidden entry to church. He took his woes to God. 'They won't let me in, Lord, because I am a sinner.'

'What are you complaining about?' said God. 'They won't let Me in either.'
—Brennan Manning

Loneliness is my least favorite thing about life. The thing that I'm most worried about is just being alone without anybody to care for or someone who will care for me.

—Anne Hathaway

Loneliness expresses the pain of being alone and solitude expresses the glory of being alone.
—Paul Tillich

The eternal quest of the individual human being is to shatter his loneliness.

—Norman Cousins

LOVE

I will sing of steadfast love and justice; to You, O Lord, I will make music.

—Psalm 101:1 KJB

If you could only love enough, you could be the most powerful person in the world.
—Emmet Fox

Love all, trust few, do wrong to none.
—William Shakespeare

All the love we come to know in life springs from the love we knew as children.
—Thomas J. Langley

While there are illegitimate parents, there are no illegitimate children.
—Rick Warren

Kids go where there is excitement. They stay where there is love.
—Ralph Waldo Emerson

The most important thing that parents can teach their child is how to get along without them.
—Frank A. Clark

*Dads are the most ordinary men turned by love
into heroes, adventurers, story-tellers, singers of
songs.*

—Pam Brown

*Husbands, love your wives, just as Christ loved
the church, and gave Himself up for her.*
—Ephesians 5:25 NIV

*Having God's unconditional love does not mean
you have God's unconditional approval.*
—Miles McPherson

*To have found God and still to pursue Him is the
soul's paradox of love.*
—A. W. Tozer

God loves each of us as if there was only one of us.
—St. Augustine

*I really only love God as much as I love the person
I love the least.*
—Dorothy Day

*Do what you love in the service of people who
love what you do.*
—Steve Farber

*If having a soul means being able to feel love and
loyalty and gratitude, than animals are better off
than a lot of humans.*
—James Herriot

A new command I give you: Love one another. As I have loved you, so you must love one another.
—John 13:34 NIV

Love means giving up—yielding my preferences, comfort, goals, security, money, energy or time for the benefit of someone else.
—Rick Warren

Riches take wings, comforts vanish, hope withers away, but love stays with us. Love is God.
—Lew Wallace

God loves people because of who God is, not because of who we are.
—Philip Yancey

Every time you smile at someone, it is an action of love, a gift to that person, a beautiful thing.
—Mother Teresa

When things go bad it drives you into God and you develop a poise, a power, a strong kind of joy that never goes away.
—Timothy J. Keller

I cannot think that we are useless or God would not have created us. There is one God looking down on us all. We are all the children of one God. The sun, the darkness, the winds are all listening to what we have to say.
—Geronimo

Since you and your wife are one flesh, what you think and feel of your wife reflects back to your soul. She can read your unconscious thoughts when you sleep.
—John M. Mooney

Love does not dominate; it cultivates.
—Johann Wolfgang
von Goethe

Love isn't something you find. Love is something that finds you.
—Loretta Young

No one has ever loved anyone the way everyone wants to be loved.
—Mignon McLaughlin

Most of mankind's misery stems from feeling unloved.
—Sara Young

The best use of life is love. The best expression of love is time. And the best time to love is now.
—Rick Warren

True prayer is only another name for the love of God.
—François Fénelon

Do what you love in the service of people who love what you do.
—Steve Farber

Love does not consist in gazing at each other, but in looking outward together in the same direction.
—Antoine de Saint-
Exupéry

Sometimes the heart sees what is invisible to the eye.
—H. Jackson Brown Jr.

Those who truly love us will never knowingly ask us to be other than where we are.
—Mark Nepo

Lord, grant that I might not so much seek to be loved as to love.
—St. Francis of Assisi

Until one has loved an animal, a part of one's soul remains unawakened.
—Anatole France

You don't have to go looking for love when it's where you come from.
—Werner Erhard

Love is the only force capable of transforming an enemy into a friend.
—Martin Luther King Jr.

The desire to feel love is the last illusion; let it go and you will be free.
—Margaret Atwood

MERCY

Have mercy on us, Lord, have mercy on us, for we have endured no end of contempt.
                                        —Psalm 123:3 NIV

Mercy is the golden chain by which society is bound together.
                                        —William Blake

God's mercy is fresh and new every morning.
                                        —Joyce Meyer

Mercy has converted more souls than zeal, or eloquence, or the learning of all of them.
                                        —Søren Kierkegaard

Church is a place where I can say unashamedly, 'I don't need to sin, I need another sinner.'
                                        —Philip Yancey

It is not what you are nor what you have been that God sees with His all merciful eyes, but what you desire to be.
                                        —Anonymous -
                                        The Cloud of Unknowing

For Christ dwells only in sinners.
                                        —Martin Luther

Cowards are cruel, but the brave love mercy and delight to save.

—John Gay

For God so loved the world that He gave His one and only Son, that whoever believes in Him shall not perish but have eternal life.

—John 3:16 NIV

I am with you, I am for you, I am in you. I expect more failure from you than you expect from yourself.

—Brennan Manning

Lord Jesus, Son of God, have mercy on me, a sinner.

—The Jesus Prayer

Lord Jesus, Son of God, thank you for having mercy on me, a sinner—Lord Jesus, Son of God, thank you for having mercy on me, a child of yours, who at times sins.

—John M. Mooney

Many people cannot be filled with the Holy Spirit until they are empty.

—Dwight L. Moody

I am the most noteworthy sinner, but I have cried out to the Lord for grace and mercy, and they have covered me completely. I have found the sweetest consolation since I made it my whole purpose to enjoy His marvellous Presence.

—Christopher Columbus

I don't want to be at the mercy of my emotions. I want to use them, to enjoy them, and to dominate them.

—Oscar Wilde

Human judges can show mercy. But against the laws of nature, there is no appeal.

—Arthur C. Clarke

Nothing can make injustice just but mercy.

—Robert Frost

We shall show mercy, but we shall not ask for it.

—Winston Churchill

A dark cloud is no sign that the sun has lost his light; and dark black convictions are no arguments that God has laid aside His mercy.

—Charles H. Spurgeon

God tolerates even our stammering, and pardons our ignorance whenever something inadvertently escapes us—as, indeed, without this mercy there would be no freedom to pray.

—John Calvin

The angel of mercy, the child of love, together had flown to the realms above.

—Fanny Crosby

God's mercy and grace give me hope—for myself, and for our world.

—Billy Graham

OBEDIENCE

A song of ascents. Blessed are all who fear the Lord, who walk in obedience to Him.
—Psalm 128:1 NIV

Only the believing obey; only the obedient believe.
—Dietrich Bonhoeffer

To shun one's cross is to make it heavier.
—Henri Frédéric Amiel

For God, no cost is too high.
—Watchman Nee

Obedience is the fruit of faith.
—Christina Rossetti

It is not hard to obey when we love the one whom we obey.
—St. Ignatius

Obedience keeps the rules. Love knows when to break them.
—Anthony de Mello

Every parent knows that delayed obedience is really disobedience.
—Rick Warren

When obedience ceases to be an irritant and becomes our quest, in that moment God will endow us with power.
—Ezra Taft Benson

God uses imperfect people for impossible tasks.
—John Paul Warren

A person prays, that he himself may be constructed, not that God may be instructed.
—St. Augustine

One act of obedience is better than one hundred sermons.
—Dietrich Bonhoeffer

Rebellion to tyrants is obedience to God.
—William Penn

The Law never finds righteousness; it only confirms unrighteousness. The Gospel never finds righteousness, it only gives and bestows righteousness.
—C. F. W. Walther

Things non-essential to salvation are nonetheless essential to obedience.
—Charles H. Spurgeon

Because one person disobeyed God, many became sinners. But because one other person obeyed God, many will be made righteous.
—Romans 5:19 NLT

A great work is made out of a combination of obedience and liberty.
> —Nadia Boulanger

Wilt thou seal up the avenues of ill? Pay every debt as if God wrote the bill.
> —Ralph Waldo Emerson

God's promises are all on condition of humble obedience.
> —Ellen G. White

One only has the choice between God and idolatry.
> —Simone Weil

To be properly wicked, you don't have to break the law, just follow it to the letter.
> —Anthony de Mello

As a result of your ministry, they will give glory to God. For your generosity to them and to all believers will prove that you are obedient to the Good News of Christ.
> —2 Corinthians 9:13 NLT

The willing, Destiny guides them. The unwilling, Destiny drags them.
> —Lucius Anneaus Seneca

Obedience of the law is demanded; not asked as a favor.
> —Theodore Roosevelt

You will seek Me, and will not find Me; where I am, you cannot come.
> —John 7:34 ESV

There are only two kinds of people in the end: those who say to God, 'Thy will be done,' and those to whom God says, 'All right then, have it your way.'
> —C. S. Lewis

Obedience unlocks God's power.
> —Rick Warren

There will be no peace in any soul until it is willing to obey the voice of God.
> —Dwight L. Moody

If God creates a world of particles and waves, dancing in obedience to mathematical and physical laws, who are we to say that He cannot make use of those laws to cover the surface of a small planet with living creatures?
> —Martin Gardner

A boy can learn a lot from a dog: obedience, loyalty, and the importance of turning around three times before lying down.
> —Robert Benchley

Through the grace of Christ we shall live in obedience to the law of God written upon our hearts. Having the spirit of Christ, we shall walk even as He walked.
> —Ellen G. White

PAIN

He heals the brokenhearted and binds up their wounds.

—Psalm 147:3 NIV

We must all suffer one of two things: the pain of discipline or the pain of regret or disappointment.

—Jim Rohn

Take chances, make mistakes. That's how you grow. Pain nourishes your courage. You have to fail in order to practice being brave.
—Mary Tyler Moore

If there is no self then whose arthritis is this?
—Jewish Buddha

Turn your wounds into wisdom.
—Oprah Winfrey

Illness does not crush a person under the weight of their 'mortal body,' but to the contrary, turns the person toward God.
—Jean-Claude Larchet

Pain is no evil, unless it conquers us.
—Charles Kingsley

Pain tells us that we have to put our survival onto something that is a violation of some principle of consciousness.

—David R. Hawkins

All grief—no matter what the occasion—is for self.

—Anthony de Mello

The only place outside Heaven where you can be perfectly safe from all the dangers and perturbations of love is Hell.

—C. S. Lewis

A man who suffers before it is necessary suffers more than is necessary.

—Lucius Annaeus Seneca

Either immediately or ultimately every dollar of government spending must be raised through a dollar of taxation. Once we look at the matter. In this way, the supposed miracles of government spending will appear in another light.

—Henry Hazlitt

Our heavenly Father understands our disappointment, suffering, pain, fear and doubt. He is always there to encourage our hearts and help us understand that He's sufficient for all of our needs. When I accepted this as an absolute truth in my life, I found that my worrying stopped.

—Charles Stanley

PEACE

Turn from evil and do good; Seek peace and pursue it. The eyes of the Lord are on the righteous, and His ears are attentive to their cry.
—Psalm 34:14 NIV

Peace begins with a smile.
—Mother Teresa

Freedom from desire leads to inner peace.
—Lao Tse

There is no path to peace. Peace is the path.
—Mahatma Gandhi

Therefore whoever desires peace, let him prepare for war.
—Flavius Vegetius Renatus

War does not determine who is right—only who is left.
—Bertrand Russell

In order for a war to be just, three things are necessary. First, the authority of the sovereign. Secondly, a just cause. Thirdly, a rightful intention.
—Thomas Aquinas

Yesterday is ashes; tomorrow wood. Only today does the fire burn brightly.

—Old Eskimo Proverb

If you look at the world, you'll be distressed. If you look within, you'll be depressed. If you look at God, you'll be at rest.

—Corrie ten Boom

To forgive is the highest most beautiful form of love. In return, you will receive untold peace and happiness.

—Robert Muller

For anyone who enters God's rest also rests from their works, just as God did from His.

—Hebrews 4:10 NIV

Peace is a journey of a thousand miles and it must be taken one step at a time.

—Lyndon B. Johnson

What you leave behind is not what is engraved in stone monuments, but what is woven into the lives of others.

—Pericles

Nothing is worth more than this day. You cannot relive yesterday. Tomorrow is still beyond your reach.

—Johann Wolfgang
von Goethe

PERSEVERANCE

*Those who go out weeping, carrying seed to sow,
will return with songs of joy, carrying sheaves
with them.*

—Psalm 126:6 NIV

*People often say that motivation doesn't last.
Well, neither does bathing—that's why we recom-
mend it daily.*

—Zig Ziglar

*Motivation is what gets you started; habit is what
keeps you going.*

—Jim Rohn

*People do not decide their futures, they decide
their habits and their habits decide their futures.*

—F. Matthias Alexander

*Adversity is not simply a tool. It is God's most
effective tool for the advancement of our spiritual
lives.*

—Charles Stanley

*The battlefield for spiritual warfare is primarily
in your thought life.*

—Rick Warren

In spiritual growth, learn to expect failure.
—Henry Cloud/
John Townsend

The secret of life, though, is to fall seven times and to get up eight times.
—Paulo Coelho

Failure is only the opportunity to begin again more intelligently.
—Henry Ford

Where the determination is, the way can be found.
—George S. Clason

The productivity of work is not the responsibility of the worker but of the manager.
—Peter Drucker

There's no future in any job; the future lies in the man who holds the job.
—George Crane

Any occurrence requiring undivided attention will be accompanied by a compelling distraction.
—Robert Bloch

The three ordinary things that we often don't pay enough attention to, but which I believe are the drivers of all success, are hard work, perseverance, and basic honesty.
—Azim Pemji

Things don't go wrong and break your heart so you can become bitter and give up. They happen to break you down and build you up so you can be all that you were intended to be.
—Charles Tremendous Jones

You weren't created to be unhappy in order to keep everyone else happy. Run your own race.
—Joel Osteen

It is hard to have failed, but it is worse never to have tried to succeed.
—Theodore Roosevelt

If we don't start, it's certain we cannot arrive.
—Zig Ziglar

It is not enough that we do our best; sometimes we must do what is required.
—Winston Churchill

He who has a why to live can bear almost any how.
—Friedrich Neitzsche

Great works are performed not by strength but by perseverance.
—Samuel Johnson

Everything is perfect, and there is always room for improvement.
—Shunryu Suzuki

Even at my age, I'm trying to improve. Never give up, no matter what...Even if you get last place—finish.
—Louis Zamperini

Many people in spiritual growth become discouraged and disheartened. Remember that struggles sometimes mean you are doing something right.
—Henry Cloud/
John Townsend

The difference between the hero and coward is the hero sticks in there five minutes longer.
—Brian Tracy

Patience and perseverance have a magical effect before which difficulties disappear and obstacles vanish.
—John Quincy Adams

We are what we repeatedly do. Excellence, then, is not an act, but a habit.
—Aristotle

A river cuts through a rock, not because of its power, but because of its persistence.
—James Watkins

When you have a great and difficult task, something perhaps almost impossible, if you only work a little at a time, every day a little, suddenly the work will finish itself.
—Isak Dinesen

POWER

Great is our Lord and mighty in power; His understanding has no limits.

—Psalm 147:5 NIV

Being in power is like being a lady, if you have to tell people who you are, you aren't.

—Margaret Thatcher

Nearly all men can stand adversity, but if you want to test a man's character, give him power.

—Abraham Lincoln

The greatness of a man's power is in the measure of his surrender.

—William Booth

You lose your power not by giving it away, but by not giving it away.

—Debasish Mridha

To have what we desire is riches, but to be able to do without them is power.

—George MacDonald

I am not interested in power for power's sake, but I'm interested in power that is moral, that is right and that is good.

—Martin Luther King Jr.

Worry comes from the belief you are powerless.
—Robert Anthony

God is the electricity and we are the lamps.
—Marianne Williamson

Having a form of godliness, but denying the power thereof: from such turn away.
—2 Timothy 3:5 KJB

Power is of two kinds. One is obtained by the fear of punishment and the other by acts of love. Power based on love is a thousand more times more effective and permanent then the one derived from fear of punishment.
—Mahatma Gandhi

If you realized how powerful your thoughts are, you would never think negative thoughts.
—Peace Pilgrim

Power concedes nothing without a demand. It never did and it never will.
—Frederick Douglass

He who wishes to be obeyed must know how to command.
—Niccolo Machiavelli

All things are subject to interpretation. Whichever interpretation prevails at a given time is a function of power and not truth.
—Friedrich Neitzsche

Because power corrupts, society's demands for moral authority and character increase as the importance of the position increases.
—John Adams

Where an excess of power prevails, property of no sort is duly respected. No man is safe in his opinions, his person, his faculties, or his possessions.
—James Madison

Experience hath shewn, that even under the best forms of government those entrusted with power have, in time, and by slow operations, perverted it into tyranny.
—Thomas Jefferson

Justice and power must be brought together, so that whatever is just may be powerful, and whatever is powerful may be just.
—Blaise Pascal

Never go backward. Attempt, and do it with all your might. Determination is power.
—Charles Simmons

It is folly for a man to pray to the gods for that which he has the power to obtain by himself.
—Epicurus

Most powerful is he who has himself in his own power.
—Lucius Anneaus Seneca

PRAYER

*In my distress I prayed to the Lord and the Lord
answered me and set me free.*
>—Psalm 118:5 NLT

*The greatest tragedy in life is not unanswered
prayer, but unoffered prayer.*
>—F. B. Meyer

*Prayers are deathless. They outlive the lives of
those who uttered them.*
>—E. M. Bounds

*I need to be filled continually with the Holy Spirit,
because I leak!*
>—Dwight L. Moody

*Morning, noon, and night I cry out in my distress,
and the Lord hears my voice.*
>—Psalm 55:17 NLT

*The one concern of the devil is to keep Christians
from praying, he fears nothing from prayerless
studies, prayerless work, prayerless religion. He
laughs at our toil, he mocks our wisdom, but he
trembles when we pray.*
>—Samuel Chadwick

Pray without ceasing.
—1 Thessalonians 5:17 KJB

To be a Christian without prayer is no more possible than to be alive without breathing.
—Martin Luther

Remember, breathe prayers. Example: You are with me, Lord, I am depending on You, Lord, I belong to You, Lord, You are my God.
—Bill Gaultiere

Start your day with prayer and reading Scripture; remember, it's not about 'me.'
—John M. Mooney

To clasp your hands in prayer is the beginning of an uprising against the disorder of this world.
—Karl L. Barth

If the only prayer you ever say in your entire life is thank you, it will be enough.
—Meister Eckhart

Music is a form of prayer.
—Toru Takemitsu

When we work, we work; when we pray, God works.
—Max Lucado

If it's worth worrying about, then it's worth praying about.
—Rick Warren

The four stages of Prayer; I talk, you listen. You talk, I listen. Neither talks, both listen. Neither talks, neither listens: Silence.
—Anthony de Mello

Bringing pleasure to God is called worship.
—Rick Warren

Prayer is simply a two-way conversation between you and God.
—Billy Graham

Man's chief end is to glorify God.
—Westminster Shorter Catechism

God has no force, no demands, no conditions but prayer.
—John Foster

Christians should seek for communion with God in public worship because 'in all acts of worship, we come into God's presence.'
—Matthew Henry

Where a people pray, there is the church; and where the church is, there is never loneliness.
—Dietrich Bonhoeffer

Prayer and praise are the oars by which a man may row his boat into the deep water of the knowledge of Christ.
—Charles H. Spurgeon

I existed from all eternity and, behold, I am here; and I shall exist till the end of time, for my being has no end.

—Jackie Francois

We have to pray with our eyes on God, not on the difficulties.

—Kahlil Gibran

What most of all hinders heavenly consolation is that you are too slow in turning yourself to prayer.

—Thomas A. Kempis

Faith in a prayer-hearing God will make a prayer-loving Christian.

—Andrew Murray

Prayer is not learned in a classroom but in the closet.

—E. M. Bounds

Pray and look at people as souls, not as bodies, clothes or minds.

—Elizabeth Gilbert

The human species is distinctive from other animals in at least three ways. We are the only animals who work, laugh and pray.

—W. H. Auden

Prayer is where the action is.

—John Wesley

The point of prayer is not to get answers from God but to have perfect and complete oneness with Him.

—Oswald Chambers

Prayer honors God; it dishonors self. It is man's plea of weakness, ignorance, want. A plea which Heaven cannot disregard. God delights to have us pray.

—E. M. Bounds

In the same way a child cannot draw a bad picture so a child of God cannot offer a bad prayer.
—Richard Foster

This is what God wants from you: a relationship!

—Rick Warren

True whole prayer is nothing but love.
—St. Augustine

If a man can but pray he can do anything. He who knows how to overcome with God in prayer has heaven and earth at his disposal.
—Charles H. Spurgeon

Prayer does not change God, but it changes him who prays.

—Søren Kierkegaard

Prayer is man's greatest power.
—W. Clement Stone

PRIDE

In his pride the wicked man does not seek Him;
and in all his thoughts there is no room for God.
—Psalm 10:4 NIV

Self is the opaque veil that hides the face of God
from us. It can be removed only in spiritual expe-
rience, never by mere instruction.
—A. W. Tozer

You can either be a host to God, or a hostage to
your ego. It's your call.
—Wayne Dyer

Self equals ego/pride.
—John M. Mooney

The Self said to him, 'You're blaming God for
what your ego has done to you.'
—David R. Hawkins

Men never do evil so completely and cheerfully as
when they do it from a religious conviction.
—Blaise Pascal

Pride and excess bring disaster for man.
—Xun Zi

Spiritual pride is the illusion that we are competent to run our own lives, achieve our own sense of self-worth and find a purpose big enough to give us meaning in life without God.
—Timothy J. Keller

Your ego wants you to feel incomplete so you strive for external gratifications.
—John M. Mooney

Pride and lovelessness always go together.
—John Ortberg

All it takes is a word of flattery or criticism to uncover the ego.
—Anthony de Mello

I am not proud, but I am happy; and happiness blinds, I think more than pride.
—Alexandre Dumas

The main thing between you and God is not so much your sins; it's your damnable good works.
—John Henry Gerstner

The primary thought in the area of religion is— keep your eyes on God, not on people. Your motivation should not be the desire to be known as a praying person. Find an inner room in which to pray where no one even knows you are praying, shut the door, and talk to God in secret. Have no motivation other than to know your Father in heaven.

—Oswald Chambers

Pride cannot live beneath the cross! Let us sit there and learn our lesson—and then rise and carry it into practice!
>—Charles H. Spurgeon

A man's pride can be his downfall, and he needs to learn when to turn to others for support and guidance.
>—Bear Grylls

The greatest pride, or the greatest despondency, is the greatest ignorance of one's self.
>—Baruch Spinoza

The rich swell up with pride, the poor from hunger.
>—Sholom Aleichem

My pride fell with my fortunes.
>—William Shakespeare

It's a fine thing to rise above pride, but you must have pride in order to do so.
>—Georges Bernanos

There are two kinds of pride, both good and bad. 'Good pride' represents our dignity and self-respect. 'Bad pride' is the deadly sin of superiority that reeks of conceit and arrogance.
>—John C. Maxwell

I take a lot of pride in being myself. I'm comfortable with who I am.
>—James McAvoy

PROSPERITY

You will eat the fruit of your labor; blessings and prosperity will be yours.

—Psalm 128:2 NIV

In prosperity, our friends know us; in adversity, we know our friends.

—John Churton Collins

Work hard at your job, and you can make a living. Work hard on yourself and you can make a fortune.

—Jim Rohn

Security lies in our ability to produce.

—General Douglas
MacArthur

Set a goal of achieving the very highest possible return on the investment of your energies.

—Brian Tracy

Prosperity is the best protector of principle.

—Mark Twain

In the day of prosperity be joyful, but in the day of adversity consider.

—King Solomon

The misfortune of the wise is better than the prosperity of the fool.

—Epicurus

We can stand affliction better than we can prosperity, for in prosperity we forget God.

—Dwight L. Moody

Ability is a poor man's wealth.

—John Wooden

Education is an ornament in prosperity and a refuge in adversity.

—Aristotle

Not he who has much is rich, but he who gives much.

—Erich Fromm

If there's a will, prosperity can't be far behind.

—W. C. Fields

In the day of prosperity be joyful, but in the day of adversity consider.

—King Solomon

To rejoice in the prosperity of others is to partake of it.

—W. Austin

Remember that when you leave this earth, you can take with you nothing that you have received—only what you have given.

—St. Francis of Assisi

PROTECTION

You are my hiding place; You will protect me from trouble and surround me with songs of deliverance.

—Psalm 32:7 NIV

God sometimes removes a person from your life for your protection. Don't run after them.
—Rick Warren

A God wise enough to create me and the world I live in is wise enough to watch out for me.
—Philip Yancey

Nowhere, by the way, are we told to build unity. We are told simply to keep unity...Unity does not need to be created; it simply needs to be protected.
—Max Lucado

God did not create evil, just as darkness is the absence of light, evil is the absence of God.
—Albert Einstein

Don't forget in the darkness what you learned in the light.

—Joseph T. Bayly

Or let them lay hold of My protection, let them make peace with Me, let them make peace with Me.
—Isaiah 27:5 ESV

Government's first duty is to protect the people, not run their lives.
—Ronald Reagan

Who needs protection of the Bill of Rights most? The weak, the most vulnerable in society.
—Danny Kaye

Once you bring life into the world, you must protect it. We must protect it by changing the world.
—Elie Wiesel

Protection of religious freedom means considering the faiths and beliefs of everyone involved.
—Mike Quigley

Enthusiasm is the best protection in any situation. Wholeheartedness is contagious. Give yourself, if you wish to get others.
—David Seabury

The power of intuitive understanding will protect you from harm until the end of your days.
—Lao Tzu

The best protection for the people is not necessarily to believe everything people tell them.
—Demosthenes

PURITY

Truly God is good to Israel, to those who are pure in heart.

—Psalm 73:1 ESV

True beauty lies in the purity of the heart.
—Mathama Gandhi

Rare is the union of beauty and purity.
—Juvenal

Give me a child for the first seven years and you may then do what you like with him afterwards.
—Francis Xavier

I have seen children successfully surmounting the effects of an evil inheritance. That is due to purity being an inherent attribute of the soul.
—Mahatma Gandhi

Blessed are the pure in heart, for they shall see God. This sentence alone would save mankind if all books and prophets were lost.
—Swami Vivekananda

The purest and most thoughtful minds are those which love color the most.
—John Ruskin

Sanctification is the real change in man from the sordidness of sin to the purity of God's image.
—William Ames

The way to preserve the peace of the church is to preserve its purity.
—Matthew Henry

Iron rusts from disuse, stagnant water loses its purity, and in cold weather becomes frozen; even so does inaction sap the vigor of the mind. So we must stretch ourselves to the very limits of human possibility. Anything less is a sin against both God and man.
—Leonardo da Vinci

If God said, 'Pick any liquid to drink for eternity,' surprisingly many people would not pick water.

—John M. Mooney

My hands are clean, but my heart has somewhat of impurity.
—Euripides

One of the standards on which your happiness is based, now and in your future, is moral purity.
—Ezra Taft Benson

Purity and simplicity are the two wings with which man soars above the earth and all temporary nature.
—Thomas à Kempis

PURPOSE

The Lord will fulfill His purpose for me; Your steadfast love, O Lord, endures forever. Do not forsake the work of Your hands.

—Psalm 138:8 ESV

The greatest tragedy in life is not death, but a life without a purpose.

—Myles Munroe

When you don't have purpose in your life, you die.
—John M. Mooney

Efforts and courage are not enough without purpose and direction.

—John F. Kennedy

The man without a purpose is like a ship without a rudder—waif, a nothing, a no man. Have a purpose in life, and, having it, throw such strength of mind and muscle into your work as God has given you.

—Thomas Carlyle

Purpose always produces passion. Nothing energizes like a clear purpose. On the other hand, passion dissipates when you lack service.

—Rick Warren

What you are is God's gift to you; what you become is your gift to God.
                                    —Hans Urs von Balthasar

God's ultimate purpose is so His Son will be exhibited in me.
                                    —Oswald Chambers

We are not human beings having a spiritual experience, we are spiritual beings having a human experience.
                                    —Pierre Teilhard
                                    de Chardin

The purpose of human life is to serve, and to show compassion and the will to help others.
                                    —Albert Schweitzer

The purpose of a life is a life of purpose.
                                    —Robert Byrne

People who use time wisely spend it on activities that advance their overall purpose in life.
                                    —John C. Maxwell

Whether the situation is as small as a meeting or as large as your whole life, the most useful question you can ask yourself is, 'What do you want to bring into being?'
                                    —Steve Chandler

If you don't know where you are going, any road will get you there.
                                    —Lewis Carroll

The secret of success is making your vocation your vacation.
— Mark Twain

Work is more fun than fun.
— Noel Coward

When you dance, your purpose is not to get to a certain place on the floor. It's to enjoy each step along the way.
— Wayne W. Dyer

There is a plan and a purpose, a value to every life, no matter what its location, age, gender or disability.
— Sharron Angle

I would argue that nothing gives life more purpose than the realization that every moment of consciousness is a precious and fragile gift.
— Steven Pinker

The purpose of our lives is to be happy.
— Dalai Lama

And in the end it's not the years in your life that count, it's the life in your years.
— Abraham Lincoln

Learn to get in touch with the silence within yourself, and know that everything in life has purpose. There are no mistakes, no coincidences, all events are blessings given to us to learn from.
— Elisabeth Kübler-Ross

REDEMPTION

He sent redemption to His people; He has commanded His covenant forever. Holy and awesome is His name!

—Psalm 111:9 ESV

The Christian faith bases everything on the extreme, self-confident nature of sin. Other faiths deal with sins—the Bible alone deals with sin.
—Oswald Chambers

You are not a sinner that sins, rather you are a child of God, a saint who at times sins. This applies to all who are in Jesus Christ.
—John M. Mooney

My home is in Heaven. I'm just traveling through this world.

—Billy Graham

Common sense dictates that without hell, there is no need for a Savior in this world or the next.
—Hank Hanegraaff

The best way to use the gold of the Redeemer is for the redemption of those in peril.
—St. Ambrose

And because you belong to Him, the power of the life-giving Spirit has freed you from the power of sin that leads to death.

—Romans 8:2 NLT

Death destroys a man, the idea of Death saves him.

—E. M. Forster

In all God's plans for human redemption, He proposes that men pray. The men are to pray in every place, in the church, in the closet, in the home, on sacred days and on secular days.

—Paddy Considine

The Bible will keep you from sin, or sin will keep you from the Bible.

—Dwight L. Moody

The gospel comprises indeed, and unfolds, the whole mystery of man's redemption, as far forth as it is necessary to be known for our salvation.

—Robert Boyle

Thank God that when Satan said in his arrogance, 'I will ascend,' Jesus said, in his humility and humanity, 'I will descend.'

—Adrian Rogers

The days misspent, the love misplaced, has inside it the seed of redemption. Nothing is exempt from resurrection.

—Kay Ryan

For the Bible says we are not only responsible for our sin, but also that we are powerless to keep from sinning...This can only lead to one conclusion: Anyone need a Savior?
—Henry Cloud/
John Townsend

Suffering is imposed on us because of sin, and it is suffering that delivers us from sin...Sin gives birth to suffering, and suffering brings death to sin.
—St. John Chrysostom

In all you do and think, are you a natural man, a child of the earth or a spiritual man, a child of God?
—John M. Mooney

Every saint has a past, and every sinner has a future.
—Oscar Wilde

You have to be a little contrite to get redemption.
—Steve Madden

Everything which is done in the present, affects the future by consequence, and the past by redemption.
—Paulo Coelho

Life is full of constant ups and downs, and all I ask for is redemption in the end.
—Robin Thicke

People find meaning and redemption in the most unusual human connections.
>—Khaled Hosseini

We cannot earn our salvation through a stellar performance and we cannot lose our salvation through a poor performance.
>—John M. Mooney

I believe in the forgiveness of sin and the redemption of ignorance.
>—Adlai E. Stevenson

Redemption comes to those who wait, forgiveness is the key.
>—Tom Petty

Redemption is not perfection. The redeemed must realize their imperfections.
>—John Piper

Redemption is possible, and it is the measure of a civilized society.
>—Greg Boyle

I have to believe there's redemption in the darkest of circumstances; otherwise it's too bleak for me.
>—Paddy Considine

People, even more than things, have to be restored, renewed, revived, reclaimed, and redeemed; never throw out anyone.
>—Audrey Hepburn

SACRIFICE

Offer the sacrifices of the righteous and trust in the Lord.

—Psalm 4:5 NIV

The natural life is not spiritual, and it can be made spiritual only by the sacrifice. If we do not resolutely sacrifice the natural, the supernatural can never be natural in us.

—Oswald Chambers

When Christ calls a man, he bids him to come and die to self.

—Dietrich Bonhoeffer

The meaning of life is to think and act like God's son, Jesus Christ.

—Mike Bennett

Without exposure to potential failure, there is no risk.

—Brennan Manning

And when He called the people unto Him with His disciples also, He said unto them, 'Whosoever will come after Me, let him deny himself, and take up his cross, and follow Me.'

—Mark 8:34 KJB

God will not look you over for medals, degrees or diplomas, but for scars.
　　　　　　　　　　　　　　—Elbert Hubbard

A pint of sweat will save a gallon of blood.
　　　　　　　　　　　　　—General George Patton

Sweat saves blood, blood saves lives, and brains save both.
　　　　　　　　　　　　　　　—Erwin Rommel

Blessed fasting subdues the demons and ultimately removes them from the combatant.
　　　　　　　　　　　　　—The Ancient Fathers
　　　　　　　　　　　　　　　of the Desert

The cross is the gate where a person enters to become one with God.
　　　　　　　　　　　　　　—John M. Mooney

I Conceive that pleasures are to be avoided if greater pains be the consequence, and pains to be coveted that will terminate in greater pleasures.
　　　　　　　　　　　　—Michel de Montaigne

Since therefore Christ suffered in the flesh, arm yourselves with the same way of thinking, for whoever has suffered in the flesh has ceased from sin.
　　　　　　　　　　　　　　　—1 Peter 4:1 ESV

True love is selfless. It is prepared to sacrifice.
　　　　　　　　　　　　　　—Sadhu Vaswani

'I indeed' was in the past, 'but He' came and something miraculous happened. Get to the end of yourself where you can do nothing but where He does everything.
—Oswald Chambers

'I hope your stay is a blessed one,' said the monk who showed the visitor to his cell. 'If you need anything let us know and we will show you how to live without it.'
—Philip Yancey

The idea of redemption is always good news, even if it means sacrifice or some difficult times.
—Patti Smith

Living is strife and torment, disappointment and love and sacrifice, golden sunsets and black storms. I said that some time ago, and today I do not think I would add one word.
—Laurence Olivier

Ethics is knowing the difference between what you have a right to do and what is right to do.
—Chief Justice
Potter Stewart

Let us sacrifice our today so that our children can have a better tomorrow.
—A. P. J. Abdul Kalam

You have to fight to reach your dream. You have to sacrifice and work hard for it.
—Lionel Messi

Self-worth

Yet You have made them a little lower than God and crowned them with glory and honor.
—Psalm 8:5 NLT

The two most important days in your life are the day you are born and the day you find out why.

—Mark Twain

Face your fears and doubts, and new worlds will open to you.
—Robert Kiyosaki

'I leave you free to be yourself.' In saying these words, you have set yourself free. You are now ready to love.
—Anthony de Mello

When your self-worth goes up, your net worth goes up with it.
—Mark Victor Hansen

When you understand that self-worth is not determined by net worth, you'll enjoy financial freedom.
—John C. Maxwell

So God created mankind in His own image, in the image of God He created them; male and female He created them.

—Genesis 1:27 NIV

But as for me, I am filled with power, with the Spirit of the Lord, and with justice and might to declare to Jacob his transgression and to Israel his sin.

—Micah 3:8 NIV

And God searches your heart, not to know what your conscious prayers are, but to find out what the prayer of the Holy Spirit is.

—Oswald Chambers

What are you using your health for, to glorify God or self?

—John M. Mooney

Every new adjustment is a crisis in self-esteem.
—Eric Hoffer

Children need models more than they need critics.

—Joseph Joubert

People seldom improve when they have no other model but themselves to copy.
—Oliver Goldsmith

You were born an original, don't die a copy.
—John Mason

SILENCE

Lord, I wait for You; You will answer, Lord my God.

—Psalm 38:15 NIV

We have been silent witnesses of evil deeds; we have been drenched by many storms; we have learnt the arts of equivocation and pretence.
—Dietrich Bonhoeffer

First they came for the Socialists, and I did not speak out—Because I was not a Socialist. Then they came for the Trade Unionists, and I did not speak out—Because I was not a Trade Unionist. Then they came for the Jews, and I did not speak out—Because I was not a Jew. Then they came for me—and there was no one left to speak for me.
—Martin Niemöller

In the end, we will remember not the words of our enemies, but the silence of our friends.
—Martin Luther King Jr.

Bad men need nothing more to compass their ends, than that good men should look on and do nothing.
—John Stuart Mill

God speaks in the silence of the heart. Listening is the beginning of prayer.
—Mother Teresa

All men's miseries derive from not being able to sit alone in a quiet room.
—Blaise Pascal

But here is the point: until I took the time to extract myself from daily routine and commit to long periods of silence, I missed hearing that internal voice. Although God may have been speaking all along, until I opened my ears it made little difference in my life.
—Philip Yancey

Those who know do not speak. Those who speak do not know.
—Lao Tzu

Don't speak unless you can improve on the silence.
—Quakers

Silence is so accurate.
—Mark Rothko

Silence is the true friend that never betrays.
—Confucius

Silence is the language of God, all else is poor translation.
—Rumi

SPIRIT

Do not cast me away from Your presence and do not take Your Holy Spirit from me.
—Psalm 51:11 NIV

Without the spirit of God, we can do nothing; we are as ships without wind, or chariots without steeds; like branches without sap, we are withered; like coals without fire we are useless.
—Charles H. Spurgeon

Being filled with the Spirit is an inside job. If you insist upon an outer experience, then you make emotions the king.
—Jack R. Taylor

Faith, it seems to me, is a matter of spirit in which there is no age. Spirit is immortality, and immortality forbids the thought of age.
—Noah Haynes Swayne

The secret of genius is to carry the spirit of the child into old age, which means never losing your enthusiasm.
—Aldous Huxley

Nature always wears the colors of the spirit.
—Ralph Waldo Emerson

Man never made any material as resilient as the human spirit.
—Bernard Williams

You don't have a soul, Doctor. You are a soul. You have a body, temporarily.
—Walter M. Miller Jr.

May the God of hope fill you with all joy and peace as you trust in Him, so that you may over-flow with hope by the power of the Holy Spirit.
—Romans 15:13 NIV

The degree of panic activity in my life is equal to the degree of my lack of personal spiritual experience.
—Oswald Chambers

A man's spirit is free, but his pride binds him with chains of suffocation in a prison of his own insecurities.
—Jeremy Aldana

Do you seek the beauty of the woman or the gentle guiding voice of the Holy Spirit?
—John M. Mooney

Through gloom and shadow look we On beyond the years! The soul would have no rainbow, Had the eyes no tears. If there is no rain there is no need for a rainbow.
—John Vance Cheney

STRENGTH

My Lord is my strength and my defense; He has become my salvation.

—Psalm 118:14 NIV

You gain strength, courage and confidence by every experience in which you really stop to look fear in the face. You are able to say to yourself, 'I have lived through this horror. I can take the next thing that comes along.' You must do the thing you think you cannot do.

—Eleanor Roosevelt

Worry does not empty tomorrow of its sorrow, it empties today of its strength.

—Corrie ten Boom

Leaders think and talk about the solutions; followers think and talk about the problems.

—Brian Tracy

There's no development physically or intellectually without effort and effort means work.

—Calvin Coolidge

Things don't wind up, they wind down if energy is not applied.

—John C. Maxwell

What gives me the most hope every day is God's grace; knowing that His grace is going to give me the strength for whatever I face, knowing that nothing is a surprise to God.
—Rick Warren

Isn't the greatest possible disaster when you are wrestling with God, not to be beaten?
—Simone Weil

If you completely give of yourself physically, you become exhausted. But when you give of yourself spiritually, you get more strength.
—Oswald Chambers

Smooth seas do not make skillful sailors.
—African Proverb

In the depth of winter, I finally learned that within me there lay an invincible summer.
—Albert Camus

Only the weak are cruel. Gentleness can only be expected from the strong.
—Leo Buscaglia

Unity is strength...when there is teamwork and collaboration, wonderful things can be achieved.
—Mattie Stepanek

That which does not kill us makes us stronger.
—Friedrich Nietzsche

SUCCESS

Please, O Lord, please save us. Please, Lord, please give us success.

—Psalm 118:25 NLT

If you have a job without aggravations, you don't have a job.

—Malcolm Forbes

Let us realize the privilege to work is a gift; that the power to work is a blessing, that the love of work is success.

—David O. McKay

Don't aim for success if you want it; just do what you love and believe in, and it will come naturally.

—David Frost

Success is not to be pursued; it is to be attracted by the person we become.

—Jim Rohn

The greatness of man is not in how much wealth he acquires, but in his integrity and his ability to affect those around him positively.

—Bob Marley

It is only as we develop others that we permanently succeed.
> —Harvey S. Firestone

Coming together is a beginning; keeping together is progress; working together is success.
> —Henry Ford

Winners are not afraid of losing. But losers are. Failure is part of the process of success. People who avoid failure also avoid success.
> —Robert Kiyosaki

To me success can only be achieved through repeated failure and introspection. In fact, success represents the 1% of your work which results from the 99% that is called failure.
> —Soichiro Honda

If you have no critics you'll likely have no success.
> —Malcolm X

One fails forward toward success.
> —Charles F. Kettering

Frustration, although quite painful at times, is a very positive and essential part of success.
> —Bo Bennett

Success is the feeling I get when I live out my values.
> —Rick Warren

There are many ways to success, not the least of which is the way your child describes you when talking to a friend.
—Grey Owl

At times many people throughout history have destroyed their souls through earthly success.
—John M. Mooney

God constantly watches your response to people, success, conflict, illness, even the weather.
—Rick Warren

Success—keeping your mind awake and your desire asleep.
—Sir Walter Scott

The price of success must be paid in full, in advance.
—Brian Tracy

Success depends on previous preparation, and without such preparation there is sure to be failure.
—Confucius

I'd rather attempt to do something great and fail than to attempt to do nothing and succeed.
—Robert H. Schuller

I never dreamed about success, I worked for it.
—Estee Lauder

A successful man is one who can lay a firm foundation with the bricks others have thrown at him.
—David Brinkley

Belief in oneself is one of the most important bricks in building any successful venture.
—Lydia M. Child

One secret of success in life is for a man to be ready for his opportunity when it comes.
—Benjamin Disraeli

Successful people ask better questions, and as a result, they get better answers.
—Tony Robbins

Capital isn't scarce; vision is.
—Sam Walton

The price of success is hard work, dedication to the job at hand, and the determination that whether we win or lose, we have applied the best of ourselves to the task at hand.
—Vince Lombardi

You must put your head into the lion's mouth if the performance is to be a success.
—Winston Churchill

Success is to be measured not so much by the position that one has reached in life as the obstacles which he has overcome.
—Booker T. Washington

THANKFULNESS

Give thanks to the Lord, for He is good! His faithful love endures forever.

—Psalm 136:1 NLT

Thankfulness is the soil in which pride does not easily grow.

—Michael Ramsey

The way to love anything is to realize that it might be lost.

—Gilbert K. Chesterton

For the glory of God is a living man; and the life of man consists in beholding God.

—St. Iraneaus

Jesus did not let him, but said, 'Go home to your own people and tell them how much the Lord has done for you, and how He has had mercy on you.'

—Mark 5:19 NIV

Expect great things from God; attempt great things for God.

—William Carey

The thankful receiver bears a plentiful harvest.

—William Blake

You will never grow a close relationship with God by just attending church once a week or even having a daily quiet time. Friendship with God is built by sharing all your life experiences with Him.

—Rick Warren

If a fellow isn't thankful for what he's got, he isn't likely to be thankful for what he is going to get.

—Frank A. Clark

If you are really thankful, what do you do? You share.

—W. Clement Stone

Thankfulness creates gratitude which generates contentment that causes peace.

—Todd Stocker

Joy is thankfulness, and when we are joyful, that is the best expression of thanks we can offer the Lord, Who delivers us from sorrow and sin.

—Thaddeus of Vitovnica

When you rise in the morning, give thanks for the light, for your life, for your strength. Give thanks for your food and for the joy of living. If you see no reason to give thanks, the fault lies in yourself.

—Tecumseh

There is no happier person than a truly thankful, content person.

—Joyce Meyer

TRUST

Let the morning bring me word of Your unfailing love, for I have put my trust in You. Show me the way I should go, for to You I entrust my life.
—Psalm 143:8 NIV

The spiritual is real. If we would rise into that region of light and power plainly beckoning us through the Scriptures of truth, we must break the evil habit of ignoring the spiritual. We must shift our interest from the seen to the unseen. For the great unseen Reality is God.
—A. W. Tozer

To have a god is to have something in which the heart entirely trusts.
—Martin Luther

One of the greatest strains in life is the strain of waiting for God.
—Oswald Chambers

God is most glorified in us when we are most satisfied in Him.
—John Piper

Don't let your hearts be troubled, trust in God, and trust also in Me.
—John 14:1 NLT

If people like you, they'll listen to you, but if they trust you they'll do business with you.
—Zig Ziglar

Trust yourself. Create the kind of self that you will be happy to live with all your life. Make the most of yourself by fanning the tiny, inner sparks of possibility into flames of achievement.
—Golda Meir

Trust but verify.
—Russian Proverb

Trust is built with consistency.
—Lincoln Chafee

If you have three people in your life you can trust, you can consider yourself the luckiest person in the whole world.
—Selena Gomez

The Bible offers us three metaphors that teach us God's view of life. Life is a test, life is a trust and life is a temporary assignment.
—Rick Warren

There is no security on this earth; there is only opportunity.
—General Douglas MacArthur

To be trusted is a greater compliment than being loved.
—George MacDonald

TRUTH

Lead me by Your truth and teach me, for You are the God who saves me. All day long I put my hope in You.

—Psalm 25:5 NLT

I never did give them hell, I just told them the truth, and they thought it was hell.
—Harry S. Truman

Hell is the greatest monument to human freedom.
—C. S. Lewis

Freedom is a fragile thing and is never more than one generation away from extinction. It is not ours by inheritance; it must be fought for and defended constantly by each generation, for it comes only once to a people. Those who have known freedom and then lost it have never known it again.

—Ronald Reagan

Satan tries to get you to doubt what God has said about the sin: Is it really wrong?...But a little sin is like being a little pregnant: It will eventually show itself.

—Rick Warren

Truth is too clear. It reveals and condemns sin.
—Pastor John MacArthur

For the wages of sin is death, but the gift of God is eternal life in Christ Jesus our Lord.
—Romans 6:23 NIV

The truth of the matter is that all we have to do is live long enough, and we will suffer.
—D. A. Carson

God is truth. All who seek truth seek God, whether this is clear to them or not.
—St. Edith Stein

For no one should consider anything his own, except perhaps a lie, since all truth is from Him who said, 'I am the truth.'
—St. Augustine

Why, then, 'tis none to you, for there is nothing either good or bad, but thinking makes it so. To me it is a prison.
—William Shakespeare

When you want to help people, you tell them the truth; when you want to help yourself, you tell them what they want to hear.
—Thomas Sowell

Three things cannot be hidden: the sun, the moon, and the truth.
—Buddha

We lie the loudest when we lie to ourselves.
—Eric Hoffer

My words, thoughts and deeds have a boomerang effect. So be—careful what you send out.
—Allan Rufus

The Mirror Principle: The first person we must examine is ourselves.
—John C. Maxwell

The discovery of truth is prevented more effectively, not by the false appearance things present and which mislead into error, not directly by weakness of the reasoning powers, but by preconceived opinion, by prejudice.
—Arthur Schopenhauer

He who has truth is in the majority, though he be one.
—Arabic Proverb

If you tell the truth, you don't have to remember anything.
—Mark Twain

Facts do not cease to exist because they are ignored.
—Aldous Huxley

Occasionally he stumbled over the truth, but hastily picked himself up and hurried on as if nothing had happened.
—Winston Churchill

Falsehood flies, and Truth comes limping after it, so that when men come to be undeceived, it is too late; the jest is over, and the tale hath had its effect.

—Jonathan Swift

Never be afraid to raise your voice for honesty and truth and compassion against injustice and lying and greed. If people all over the world... would do this, it would change the earth.

—William Faulkner

Because to take away a man's freedom of choice, even his freedom to make the wrong choice, is to manipulate him as though he were a puppet and not a person.

—Madeleine L'Engle

The past is what is real and true, while history is merely what someone recorded.

—Andy Andrews

So we fix our eyes not on what is seen, but on what is unseen, since what is seen is temporary, but what is unseen is eternal.

—2 Corinthians 4:18 NIV

Learn to live from your true center in Me. I reside in the deepest depths of your being, in eternal union with your spirit...The external world is always in flux, under the curse of death and decay. But there is a gold mine of Peace deep within you, waiting to be tapped.

—Sara Young

Where riches hold the dominion of the heart, God has lost his authority.
> —John Calvin

Science without religion is lame, religion without science is blind.
> —Albert Einstein

By doubting we are led to question, by questioning, we arrive at the truth.
> —Peter Abelard

Doubt is the incentive to truth and inquiry leadeth the way.
> —Hosea Ballou

Man is at least himself when he talks in his own person. Give him a mask, and he will tell you the truth.
> —Oscar Wilde

What we weave in time, we wear in eternity.
> —John Charles Ryle

In life, disappointments are normal, misery is not, you choose.
> —John M. Mooney

All truths are easy to understand once they are discovered; the point is to discover them.
> —Galileo Galilei

If the world was perfect, it wouldn't be.
> —Yogi Berra

UNDERSTANDING

Give me understanding, so that I may keep Your law and obey it with all my heart.
— Psalm 119:34 NIV

It is difficult to get a man to understand something when his salary depends upon his not understanding it.
— Upton Sinclair

You cannot solve a problem until you acknowledge that you have one and take responsibility for solving it.
— Zig Ziglar

A problem well put is half-solved.
— John Dewey

I don't think people understand how stressful it is to explain what's going on in your head when you don't understand it yourself.
— Sara Quin

If you correct your mind, the rest of your life will fall into place.
— Lao Tzu

Much learning does not teach understanding.
— Heraclitus

The evil that is in the world almost always comes of ignorance, and good intentions may do as much harm as malevolence if they lack understanding.

—Albert Camus

A generation which ignores history has no past—and no future.

—Robert A. Heinlein

Socialism only works in two places: Heaven where they don't need it and hell where they already have it.

—Ronald Reagan

Folks never understand the folks they hate.

—James Russell Lowell

If your relationship has enough trust, honesty and understanding, it should never require promises, terms and conditions.

—Nishan Panwar

Oh senseless man, who cannot possibly make a worm and yet will create gods by the dozen.

—Michel de Montaigne

God speaks in the language you know best—not through your ears, but through your circumstances.

—Oswald Chambers

If you are unable to serve men, how can you serve the spirits? If you do not understand life, how can you understand death?
—Confucius

Everyone hears only what he understands.
—Johann Wolfgang von Goethe

Understanding is much deeper than knowledge. There are many people who know us, but very few who understand us.
—Unknown

Be patient and understanding. Life is too short to be vengeful and malicious.
—Phillips Brooks

Nothing in life is to be feared, it is only to be understood. Now is the time to understand more, so that we may fear less.
—Marie Curie

Life can only be understood backwards; but it must be lived forward.
—Søren Kierkegaard

For me, it is far better to grasp the Universe as it really is than to persist in delusion, however satisfying and reassuring.
—Carl Sagan

Wisdom

My mouth will speak words of wisdom; the me-diation of my heart will give you understanding.
—Psalm 49:3 NIV

The only true wisdom is in knowing you know nothing.
—Socrates

Everything should be as simple as it can be, but not simpler.
—Albert Einstein

Leave your simple ways and you will live; walk in the way of insight.
—Proverbs 9:6 NIV

It is the heart which perceives God and not the reason. That is what faith is: God perceived by the heart, not by the reason.
—Blaise Pascal

Where is the Life we have lost in living? Where is the wisdom we have lost in knowledge? Where is the knowledge we have lost in information? The cycles of heaven in twenty centuries bring us far-ther from God and nearer to the Dust.
—T. S. Eliot

Attachment to spiritual things is therefore just as much an attachment as inordinate love of everything else.

—Thomas Merton

Great spirits have always encountered violent opposition from mediocre minds. The mediocre mind is incapable of understanding the man who refuses to bow blindly to conventional prejudices and chooses instead to express his opinions courageously and honestly.

—Albert Einstein

The Lord works from the inside out. The world works from the outside in. The world would take people out of the slums. Christ takes the slums out of people, and then they take themselves out of the slums.

—Ezra Taft Benson

Knowledge comes but wisdom lingers, and he bears a laden breast, Full of sad experience, moving toward the stillness of his rest.

—Alfred Lord Tennyson

Wisdom ceases to be wisdom when it becomes too proud to weep, too grave to laugh, and too selfish to seek other than itself.

—Kahlil Gibran

Learn to say 'no' to the good, so you can say 'yes' to the best.

—John C. Maxwell

Statistics are no substitute for judgment.
—Henry Clay

A wise and frugal government, which shall re-strain men from injuring one another, shall leave them otherwise free to regulate their own pursuits of industry and improvement, and shall not take from the mouth of labor the bread it has earned.
—Thomas Jefferson

Politics is supposed to be the second oldest profession. I have come to realize that it bears a very close resemblance to the first.
—Ronald Reagan

By three methods we may learn wisdom: First, by reflection, which is noblest; second, by imitation, which is easiest; and third by experience, which is the bitterest.
—Confucius

The wise store up choice food and olive oil, but fools gulp theirs down.
—Proverbs 21:20 NIV

We are not made wise by the recollection of our past, but by the responsibility of our future.
—George Bernard Shaw

Wisdom we know is the knowledge of good and evil, not the strength to choose between the two.
—John Cheever

It's better to walk alone, than with a crowd going in the wrong direction.
　　　　　　　　　　　—Diane Grant

The hardest thing in life to learn is which bridge to cross and which to burn.
　　　　　　　　　　　—David Russell

The pessimist complains about the wind; the optimist expects it to change, the realist adjusts the sails.
　　　　　　　　　　　—William Arthur Ward

Ignorant men raise questions that wise men answered a thousand years ago.
　　　　　　　　　　　—Johann Wolfgang
　　　　　　　　　　　von Goethe

Assumptions can affect Observation. Observation breeds Conviction. Convention produces Experience. Experience generates Behavior, which, in turn, confirms Assumptions.
　　　　　　　　　　　—Anthony de Mello

The more sand that has escaped from the hourglass of our life, the clearer we should see through it.
　　　　　　　　　　　—Jean Paul

The more you like yourself, the less you are like anyone else, which makes you unique.
　　　　　　　　　　　—Walt Disney

The problem with beauty is that it's like being born rich and getting poorer.
—Joan Collins

It's not what you look at that matters, it's what you see.
—Henry David Thoreau

Life is a traveling to the edge of knowledge, then a leap is taken.
—D. H. Lawrence

True wisdom comes to each of us when we realize how little we understand about life, ourselves, and the world around us.
—Socrates

A loving heart is the truest wisdom.
—Charles Dickens

Do not try to live forever. You will not succeed.
—George Bernard Shaw

All that is not eternal is eternally out of date.
—C. S. Lewis

To finish the moment, to find the journey's end in every step of the road, to live the greatest number of good hours, is wisdom.
—Ralph Waldo Emerson

Conclusion

I sincerely hope you enjoyed this eclectic and inspiring collection. I would like to conclude by sharing a short vignette from one of my favorite authors, Anthony de Mello, and a prayer that is very special to me.

It intrigued the congregation to see their rabbi disappear each week on the eve of the Sabbath. They suspected he was secretly meeting the Almighty, so they deputed one of their number to follow him.

This is what the man saw: the rabbi disguised himself in peasant clothes and served a paralyzed Gentile woman in her cottage, cleaning out the room and preparing a Sabbath meal for her.

When the spy got back, the congregation asked, 'Where did the rabbi go? Did he ascend to heaven?'

'No,' the man replied. 'He went even higher.'
—Anthony de Mello

Teach me, my Lord, to be sweet and gentle in all the events of life: in disappointments, in the thoughtlessness of others, in the insincerity of those I trusted, in the unfaithfulness of those upon whom I relied.

Let me put myself aside, to think of the happiness of others, to hide my little pains and heartaches, so that I may be the only one to suffer them. Teach me to profit by the suffering that comes across my path.

Let me so use it that it may mellow me, not harden nor embitter me; that it may make me patient, not irritable, that it may make me broad in my forgiveness, not narrow, haughty and overbearing.

May no one be less good for having come within my influence; no one less pure, less noble for having been a fellow-traveller in our journey toward Eternal Life.

As I go my rounds from one distraction to another, let me whisper, from time to time, a word of love to Thee. May my life be lived in the supernatural, full of power for good, and strong in its purpose of sanctity. Amen.

—Catholic Prayer